Teaching Africa

EXPLORATIONS OF EDUCATIONAL PURPOSE

Volume 9

Founding Editor

Joe Kincheloe (1950-2008)

Series Editors

Shirley R. Steinberg, *McGill University, Montreal, Quebec, Canada*
Kenneth Tobin, *City University of New York, USA*

Editorial Board

Barrie Barrell, *Memorial University of Newfoundland, Canada*
Rochelle Brock, *University of Indiana, Gary, USA*
Stephen Petrina, *University of British Columbia, Canada*
Christine Quail, *State University of New York, Oneonta, USA*
Nelson Rodriguez, *College of New Jersey, USA*
Leila Villaverde, *University of North Carolina, Greensboro, USA*
John Willinsky, *Stanford University, USA*

Series Scope

In today's dominant modes of pedagogy, questions about issues of race, class, gender, sexuality, colonialism, religion, and other social dynamics are rarely asked. Questions about the social spaces where pedagogy takes place - in schools, media, and corporate think tanks - are not raised. And they need to be.

The *Explorations of Educational Purpose* book series can help establish a renewed interest in such questions and their centrality in the larger study of education and the preparation of teachers and other educational professionals. The editors of this series feel that education matters and that the world is in need of a rethinking of education and educational purpose.

Coming from a critical pedagogical orientation, *Explorations of Educational Purpose* aims to have the study of education transcend the trivialization that often degrades it. Rather than be content with the frivolous, scholarly lax forms of teacher education and weak teaching prevailing in the world today, we should work towards education that truly takes the unattained potential of human beings as its starting point. The series will present studies of all dimensions of education and offer alternatives. The ultimate aim of the series is to create new possibilities for people around the world who suffer under the current design of socio-political and educational institutions.

For further volumes:
http://www.springer.com/series/7472

George J. Sefa Dei

Teaching Africa

Towards a Transgressive Pedagogy

George J. Sefa Dei
University of Toronto
Ontario Institute for Studies in
  Education (OISE)
252 Bloor Street W.
Toronto ON
M5S 1V6
george.dei@utoronto.ca

ISBN 978-1-4020-5770-0 (hardcover)   e-ISBN 978-1-4020-5771-7
ISBN 978-94-007-2861-5 (softcover)
DOI 10.1007/978-1-4020-5771-7
Springer Dordrecht Heidelberg London New York

Library of Congress Control Number: 2009940148

© Springer Science+Business Media B.V. 2010, First softcover printing 2012
No part of this work may be reproduced, stored in a retrieval system, or transmitted in any form or by any means, electronic, mechanical, photocopying, microfilming, recording or otherwise, without written permission from the Publisher, with the exception of any material supplied specifically for the purpose of being entered and executed on a computer system, for exclusive use by the purchaser of the work.

Printed on acid-free paper

Springer is part of Springer Science+Business Media (www.springer.com)

This work is dedicated to the late Joe Kincheloe for his intellectual kindness, love of life, and his untiring efforts and devotion to inspire the critical work of minority scholars to gain a footing in the corridors of dominant publishing circles.

Foreword

One is always struck by the brilliant work of George Sefa Dei but nothing so far has demonstrated his pedagogical leadership as much as the current project. With a sense of purpose so pure and so thoroughly intellectual, Dei shows why he must be credited with continuing the motivation and action for justice in education. He has produced in this powerful volume, *Teaching Africa*, the same type of close reasoning that has given him credibility in the anti-racist struggle in education.

Sustaining the case for the democratization of education and the revising of the pedagogical method to include Indigenous knowledge are the twin pillars of his style. A key component of this new science of pedagogy is the crusade against any form of hegemonic education where one group of people assumes that they are the masters of everyone else. Whether this happens in South Africa, Canada, United States, India, Iraq, Brazil, or China, Dei's insights suggest that this hegemony of education in pluralistic and multi-ethnic societies is a false construction. We live pre-eminently in a world of co-cultures, not cultures and sub-cultures, and once we understand this difference, we will have a better approach to education and equity in the human condition.

What I have always appreciated in the work of George Sefa Dei is what I appreciate in this book: his impeccable optimism as indicated in the fact that he deems equity and justice to be possible. It is not only the possibility of these virtues existing in the society that concerns Dei, but also his commitment to demonstrating the necessity of this optimistic stance towards hegemony as the coin of good neighbourliness.

Dei is prophetic in ways that no other educational philosopher has been. He is not a bombastic voice crying out in some lonely wilderness to anyone who will listen to him. He is not an irrational foe of everything that has gone on before him, but rather he is a sober and pedantic scholar who sees the evidences and results of a globalized and hegemonic Eurocentric educational process that has served to "dumb down" a massive amount of children and adults. We are victims of this educational globalization sold on the mass markets of the world as the sole commodity to save social, political, or economic health in societies.

As globalization has increasingly revealed itself to be a part of the ongoing process of the hegemony of those who hold both military and economic power, because with such power the Eurocentric elite have been able to commodify education and to make a world where everything becomes a product. The reality is that Africa has suffered in such a construction of reality. Our educational systems have not worked for the interest of Africa but for the interests of Europe. Children in some French-speaking areas of Africa who still learn that their ancestors are the Gauls are scarred for life. They spend a considerable amount of time cleansing their brains of this type of education meant for the white colonialist children, but yet African children are victims of it. One can find books written in English that still teaches that Mungo Parks discovered the Niger River. These are a few examples, which are not trivial by any means, but examples that conceal a much bigger problem: the assumptions of knowledge and information are only Eurocentric.

One of the reasons we have not been able to ensure our children a competitive edge is because we have lacked the courage to reconstruct the curricula of Africa. George Sefa Dei is the bold challenger of the system that we have been waiting for to disturb our minds, to create dissonance about our process, and to respect those values that are worthy of respect. Dei is not claiming that everything African is good and everything European is bad; no, he is claiming that Africans must interrogate African cultural forms and systems in order to discover the best road out of the chaos and confusion of teaching African children to know more about the European culture than they know about their own culture. No other continent or people have seen such violation of traditions and values as Africa and Africans.

This is precisely the reason Dei opened his book with the idea that history has been a tool of colonialism. If you want to maintain power and control over people you have to teach them that your information and knowledge are more valuable than theirs. You have to create ways to accredit the subjects who support the system over those who do not support the colonial system. You also have to have an established cadre of individuals who believe that it is more important to carry out the mandates of the colonials than to investigate one's own culture. The issue is often resource management and the fact that long after the colonials have left physically they retain their power in images, institutions, and an entire coterie of the most loyal African Eurocentrists. They do not understand that they are not only mis-educating the children but continuing the mental enslavement of the people. Afrocentric education is not racist education; it is the fundamental right of African people, as with other people, to commence the education of children from the standpoint of Africans as subjects of their own history. We are no less agents of transformation in our historical experiences as other people. We must regain our own footing and teach our children the value of knowing the intellectual traditions of Africa. For so long Europe took its own specific, narrow, and provincial way of the world as if it were universal and imposed it upon Africa; that was racist. There is no imposition on the rest of the world in Dei's conception; he is only interested in how we go about educating African children.

What Dei and his colleagues have always encouraged us to do is to interrogate, in the best terms of that word, the cultures of numerous Indigenous peoples to gain some idea about how they have managed to transmit the values of character, common interest, and appreciation for what has already been achieved, and an intense belief in the future of the world. This is the objective of a careful, deliberate educational voice that seeks to provide for contemporary educators the path towards the eternal river of human truth. This is not a misplaced metaphor. The river is from long ago, and we are simply seeking to know something about how to manage our own affairs; George Sefa Dei has said that we have to examine everything to gain knowledge of longevity in our institutions and in our projects. This is the most remarkable advance about which I have read in many years in the matter of our education.

Temple University   Molefi K. Asante

Acknowledgements

Over the years, many people have influenced my intellectual growth to whom I owe a deep intellectual debt. I shall always be grateful for the love, kindness, and the giving of colleagues, friends, and family who have inspired me in my academic and political journeys. I have repeatedly spoken from the learning I have received in my interactions with my students and research work among youth. This work would not have been possible without the research contributions of Dr. Meredith Lordan, Stanley Doyle-Wood, and Arlo Kempf of the Ontario Institute for Studies in Education of the University of Toronto (OISE/UT). The research contributions of Arlo for chapters 1 and 2, and Stanley for chapter 5 were central to the completion of this work. Meredith spent many hours to get this entire work in shape and I shall forever remain grateful. Thank you to Marlon Simmons also for doing a quick read through of the manuscript and fixing the corrections to the galleys. I would like to thank the late Dr. Joe Kincheloe. I know he is happy where he is about my continuing work. I also want to express thanks to Shirley Steinberg for continuing where Joe left off and supporting my work. I am grateful to my family – Nana Adwo Oku-Ampofo, Ernest, Prince, Joyce, Helena, and, the rock, Agnes Koduah for always being there for me.

Toronto, Ontario George J. Sefa Dei
May 2009

Contents

Foreword vii
Introduction xvii

1 **History as Tool of Colonialism** 1
  1.1 Introduction 1
      1.1.1 Oral History and Learning and Teaching Africa 2
      1.1.2 Learning and Teaching Africa Through Written History . . 3
      1.1.3 Learning and Teaching Africa: Archaeological
           Evidence, Anthropology, Linguistics, and Science 4
  1.2 History and Its Connection to Politics, Culture, and Power 4
      1.2.1 Test: Evaluation/Assessment 9
  1.3 Conclusion 12
  References 13

2 **Teaching and Learning African History** 15
  2.1 Introduction 15
  2.2 Making the Case for African-Centred Education: The
      Roots and Place of African-Centredity 19
  2.3 African-Canadians in History 22
  2.4 Conclusion 30
  References 31

3 **The Study of Africa and the African Experience: The
Challenge and Possibilities of an Integrative Theory** 33
  3.1 Introduction 33
  3.2 The African-Centred Educational Philosophy as Anticolonial . . . 37
  References 44

4 **Theorizing Africa Beyond Its Boundaries** 47
  4.1 Introduction 47
  4.2 Re-conceptualizing Pan-Africanism Today 49
  4.3 Historical Influences 52
  4.4 Pedagogic Possibilities and Implications for Black/African Education 54
  4.5 The Possibilities of Anti-colonial Education 57

	4.6 Contesting and Engaging the Future Through Unity and Community Building	58
	References	59
5	**Teaching Africa: "Development" and Decolonization**	**61**
	5.1 Introduction	61
	5.2 The Problem with "African Development"	62
	5.3 Development as Eurocentric Paradigmatic Way of Knowing	64
	5.4 Teaching Africa: Chabal and the Power of Eurocentricity	65
	5.5 Afrocentrism in – and Is – Us	67
	5.6 Teaching African in a Global Context	68
	References	70
6	**Reclaiming "Development" Through Indigenity and Indigenous Knowledge**	**73**
	6.1 Introduction	73
	6.2 Indigenous Knowledge, Schooling, Education and African Development: Connecting the Dots	80
	6.3 African Proverbs, Folktales and Stories: Pedagogic and Instructional Relevance in the Promotion of Moral and Character Education	80
	6.4 Traditional Medicine	84
	6.5 Conclusion	85
	References	86
7	**Indigenous Knowledge! Any One? Pedagogical Possibilities for Anti-colonial Education**	**89**
	7.1 Introduction	89
	7.2 Revealing Biases Within	91
	7.3 Situating the "Political Project": Our Collective Responsibility	93
	7.4 Indigenous Knowledge: Towards a Conceptualization and Operationalization	95
	7.5 Politics of Identity and the Search for Epistemological Equity	98
	7.6 Towards a Critical Indigenous Discursive Framework	100
	7.7 Indigenous Knowledges Today: Pedagogic Possibilities for Anti-colonial Education	103
	References	105
8	**Politicizing the Contemporary Learner: Implications for African Schooling and Education**	**107**
	8.1 Introduction: On Identity and Community	107
	8.2 The Power of "Critical Education"	108
	8.3 Connecting Religion, Identity, Community, and Critical Education: The Search for Educational Options/Alternatives	109
	8.4 A Question of Language	111
	8.5 African-Centred School and the Moral Panic	111

	8.6 Conclusion	115
	References	116
9	**Looking to the Future – African-Centred Schooling in Action: Applying Development Discourse to Sustainability, Community Empowerment, and Health Awareness**	117
	9.1 Introduction: Towards an Anti-colonial Prism of Development	117
	9.2 Sustainability as Political and Intellectual Project	119
	9.3 Rethinking Sustainability: The Quest for Education for Sustainability	122
	9.4 Building Healthy and Sustainable Communities: The Challenges and Possibilities	124
	9.5 Looking Forward to Reframe Development	125
	References	126
Index		129

Introduction

1 Teaching and Learning Africa: An Introduction to Transgressive Pedagogy

I want to contribute to opening Africa – and African ways of thinking and doing – to you.

This book is written largely from the perspective of an African-centred knowledge base and educational practice. It utilizes an anti-colonial discursive pedagogy: a theorization of colonial and neocolonial relations and the implications of imperial structures on knowledge production and use; the understanding of Indigenity; and the pursuit of agency, resistance and subjective politics. Ultimately, though, it is a book about reclaiming and claiming new educational spaces for African-centred knowledges, identities, and realities to emerge. It is a book about seeing our place – our identities and responsibilities – within these educational spaces.

In this context, I use "colonial" not in the conventional sense of "foreign" and "alien", but more importantly, as "imposed and dominating". This view of "colonial" allows us to see how colonialism is domesticated and how those who have been oppressed by dominant/hegemonic discourses may find it difficult to step out of it and/or even to challenge/resist it. The book is a call to challenge dominant knowledge about Africa in order to help the contemporary learner come to grips with the challenges and possibilities of knowing about the African world and the African human condition. Critical teaching is a form of decolonization. Beyond questioning imperial, colonial, and oppressive knowledges, we need to subvert the cultural, symbolic, and political practices that render difference unimportant. The book challenges the fixed definitions and interpretations of Africa, preferring a much more dynamic presentation of the knowledge and political possibilities it offers. The book seeks to achieve these ends in the following ways:

- uses an Anti-colonial discursive platform to address distorted Eurocentric views of Africa;
- raises questions about teaching methods and methodologies relating to Africa, by addressing the pedagogic, instructional, and communicative need and urgency of what it means to critically teach about Africa;

- discusses African Indigenous knowledges and what the rest of the world can learn from these knowledges, and how to present problems such as HIV/AIDS, genocide, poverty, and human exploitation to reflect larger international issues such as the legacy of colonialisms, and the enslavement of African peoples.

This book takes an important philosophical and pedagogic position. It stresses that the teaching and learning of Africa by the contemporary student and educator of African culture, history, language, religion, political economy, and development must approach the subject matter through an Afroscopic lens or an African-centred perspective. For many youth in Euro-American schooling contexts, particularly Black youth, this is significant since the African-centred knowledge base stresses the importance of Africa and the links to the Diaspora as an intellectual exercise to affirm the students' sense of pride in their histories, myriad identities, and social, cultural, and political achievements. Even to this day many students in our school systems are continually contending with the denigration and devaluation of African culture, history, and development. There is a correlation between seeing Africa today as a "basket case" and the devaluing of the Black and African peoples' experiences in Euro-American context. Black students have been asked to repeatedly amputate a part of their history and connections to Africa on the naïve idea that the present generation of youth have no connection to Africa! How can we discuss the issues of the Diaspora without a connection to Africa and vice versa? For Africa to matter to the learner, as we consider this basic premise, educators must start to teach Africa critically in order for learning to happen.

A nagging intellectual problem that most students of Africa have to deal with is the oversimplification and over-romanticization of Africa, in terms of the challenges, opportunities, and problems confronting the continent and its peoples. This book will take an approach to Africa that goes beyond the continent and connect the missing dots. I am interested in the exploration of African issues that cross boundaries and implicate all peoples of African descent and beyond. In this context, Diasporian connections are equally important as what pertains within the continent. Africa defies simplistic analysis and interpretations. If Africa had simple problems, challenges, and solutions, then opportunities for resuscitating itself would not preoccupy minds for a long while. My optimism encourages me to think that students of Africa or any one who cares to develop a sympathetic understanding of the continent can muster the courage to confront the complexities, challenges, and opportunities offered by this geographical space. Africa is a place of study – teaching and learning among a people. Through their cultures and histories the pessimism of the intellect will be overturned.

Discussions in this book will centre on a critical exploration of the theory and practice of teaching and learning about Africa, African peoples, and the implications for schooling and education in Diasporic contexts. With the settlement of Africans around the world as a result of the Diaspora, this variety allows for multiple experiences of African-awareness to emerge. There are many questions for critical intellectual engagement: How best to address distorted Eurocentric views of Africa, including White racism toward Africa, its peoples, and the African Diasporas? What are the multiple knowledge systems in Africa? How to teach these systems in contemporary North American schools? My political and academic project is to stress the importance of Africa as a key educational issue in the twenty first century. In teaching and learning about Africa, a major concern is what the contemporary student needs to know about Africa, its importance in the international community, current neocolonial struggles, and the impact of globalization and transnational capitalism. The learning objective is to show how these issues affect Africa today and how Africa affects the world. For the educator the objective is to uncover how the interests and issues about Africa, including contemporary challenges and knowledge systems, can shape the development of curricula and critical instruction in diverse schooling settings.

At the theoretical level the discussion raises some useful questions about teaching methods and methodologies relating to Africa. In order to identify particular teaching strategies that make for the creation of relevant knowledges on Africa, we must begin by addressing the pedagogic, instructional, and communicative needs of what it means to teach about Africa in critically informed ways. Let me state from the onset that I am not concerned with the specifics of teaching tools. Instead, the discussion focuses on philosophical questions. One must first understand the philosophical basis of what we do if our educational/teaching practice is to be effective at all. I do agree theory cannot stand in opposition to what is pragmatic; we need to have theory and practice working together.

In penning down my thoughts, I have reflected on some issues from my graduate teaching experience. Over the years, I have repeatedly witnessed at least three major concerns that emerge from the students with interests in Africa. The first is around the processes of [in]validation and [de]legitimation of knowledges – how knowledges are produced and disseminated nationally/globally. Students have often queried why and how is it that certain knowledges count more so than other ways of knowing. There is a realization on the part of learners that knowledge is applied differently given local histories, environments, and contexts. Unfortunately, the processes of validating knowledges fail to take into account the many ways of knowing that can speak to the diversity of the histories of ideas and events that have shaped and continue to shape human growth and development. In questioning the hierarchy of knowledges, learners also allude to the problematic position of neutral, apolitical knowledge. In our teaching of African studies we must lay bare and grasp the processes through which, for example, Western science knowledge positions itself as a neutral, universal, and non-hegemonic way of knowing.

The second concern is the role of Indigenous/local knowledge in understanding Africa and to help rupture the dominance of certain forms of knowledges. Indigenous knowledge is perceived here as knowledge "accumulated by a group of people, not necessarily Indigenous, who by centuries of unbroken residence develop an in-depth understanding of their particular place in their particular world" (Roberts 1998: 58). The common sense ideas and cultural resources of local peoples concerning everyday realities are significant. This knowledge refers to those whose authority resides in origin, place history, and ancestry. Through these forms of knowledge in the academy (schools, colleges, and universities), educators and learners can open spaces for knowledge. For students, the role of Indigenous Knowledges in a Western academy is to serve in a project of decolonization: the active questioning and dismantling of colonial thinking and structures (see Semali and Kincheloe 1999; Dei 2000; Dei et al. 2000; Smith 1999; Yankah 2004).

The third major concern raised by students of Africa is the problematic call to "amputate" the past, culture, and community, knowing full well what Andrew Lattas (1993) says: "that the present is itself constitutive of what it is not." This posture of amputating the self, identity, and history contrasts sharply with the idea of "resistance to amputation" (Fanon 1968). The "Africa" that is present today is very much constitutive of the past. Hence, for students of Africa, it is unsettling to speak of a "post" as if we have obliterated or simplistically done away with that past and history.

These three major concerns further implicate other key questions for me: What does studying about Africa entail? What does it mean to teach Africa? What knowledges and paradigms (ways of seeing) do we employ in such undertakings? Who is producing such transgressive knowledge, how, and why? The relevance of these questions is that they have significant implications for teaching Africa. I see the implications in terms of the particular academic and political projects. I do not take the position that everyone must subscribe to these positions. But I reiterate that these positions have far-reaching implications that cannot be ignored.

2 Towards a Transgressive Pedagogy

In terms of its overarching framework let me now broach some areas critical to the teaching of Africa today (see also Dei 2003 for an abbreviated discussion).

2.1 (Re)Conceptualizing Africa

Reconceptualizing Africa calls for understanding Africa via local (African) subjects who know themselves. It also requires a sincere acknowledgement that Africa is in many ways an artificial construct and that there is power of knowledge in theorizing and teaching Africa beyond its artificial boundaries. We must also see Africa beyond homogeneity by exploring all the emerging contestations, contradictions, and ambiguities in peoples' lives. Africa is a community of difference. The politics of claiming universal sameness served well the interests of those who did not want to see Africa challenge their "stable knowledge". Difference challenges that stability and the community of sameness. There is the power of knowing difference by seeing Africa as powerfully demarcated by ethnicity, gender, class, language, culture, sexual orientation, and religion. Africa is complex, nuanced, and heterogeneous. Such acknowledgement of difference is key to appreciating the many challenges that confront the continent. It brings to the fore the fact that a one-size solution offered to Africa's problems woefully lacks a depth of knowledge about the complexities of modern-day Africa. To begin to understand, teach, and learn about Africa educators and students must understand Africa as more than a geographical space or territory. Africa is a place rich in culture and heritage, histories of struggles, successes, failures, and opportunities for moving ahead.

2.2 Beyond Particularities

Africa's complexities emerge from its diversity in terms of people, cultures, histories, and experiences. The diversity and contextual variations and differences in Africa and among her peoples and cultures must always be visible in our pedagogic practice. But acknowledging such difference and diversity in teaching and learning about Africa is not enough to understand Africa. Educators must challenge the essentializing of difference. So teaching and learning about Africa must connect the particularities and the historical specificities to their broader macro-political contexts and forces. For example, we need to see Africa within the globalized context. The "global encounter" still shapes and influences the specificities and the particular. It is always important for us to view Africa in the broader context of North-South, East-West relations. We must begin to ask where is Africa's place in contemporary global geo-politics? How do we resist the marginalization of Africa in contemporary world affairs? Africa matters fundamentally to how we construct the world. Africa's history, achievements, and contributions have served to make the global complete and whole today. We cannot dismiss these knowledges in discussions about Africa and the world. Africa is the world and the world is Africa.

2.3 Creating Relevant Knowledge

Knowledge is worth pursuing if it assists human survival and existence. The relevance of knowledge is measured not so much by what we can do with the knowledge but how such knowledge truly accounts for everyday existence. How does this knowledge offer solutions to the problems, challenges, and obstacles that confront us as a people? When I speak of "creating relevant knowledge about Africa" I gesture to the power and efficacy of teaching relevant knowledge, knowledge anchored in African people's aspirations, concerns, and needs. It is knowledge local peoples' can identify with. It is based on the philosophical position that we must understand Africa on its own terms. Richard Sklar (1993) long ago noted that those who seek to interpret Africa must develop a sympathetic understanding of African thoughts and values, as well as history and culture. Africa's history cannot be easily defined by historic periods. It is a history of the totality of lived African experiences.

Teaching Africa as a method and a means to create relevant knowledge is crucial if we are to succeed in constructing new identities outside of Euro-American ideology and dominance. It calls for developing a particular prism, one that frames issues and questions within a particular lens: "Is this in the best interests of African peoples?" We cannot take a comforting escape route which says "no one knows what is in the best interests of peoples". At least we can initiate our teaching practice by posing the relevant questions to begin with. Creating relevant knowledge begins by identifying, generating, and articulating a pedagogic theory and practice that uses lived and actual experiences of local peoples as a starting base of knowledge about Africa. Creating relevant knowledge begins by asking the right questions. Although we may not have all the answers to the questions, starting with the right questions aids the search for solutions. How is this social pursuit in the best interest of African peoples? This is a more relevant question than a bland inquisition as to "in whose interests does particular social undertaking serve?"

2.4 Collaborative Learning and Teaching

It is difficult in a world that privileges individualism and rights to ask for notions of community, interdependence, and mutual sharing of knowledge. But such a shift of the gaze is significant if we are to address what African symbolizes in the twenty first century. The enormous challenges confronting Africa and African peoples cannot be addressed within an individualist prism. This calls for initiating critical thought on issues of community development, community work, regionalism in development practice, and an engagement of the global on the basis of a solidification of ties with others with shared interests, desires, and agendas. When this gaze is turned to teaching and learning about Africa, the key challenge becomes how we pursue collaborative education.

Let us focus on teaching in this regard. I am aware of the desires and perils of collaboration at all times. Yet, I make a case for collaborative teaching on many fronts. For example, scholars share academic knowledge and pursue research from different/multi disciplines. Educators need to engage students and local communities in the process of knowledge generation. Teaching across disciplines and subject matters is another. Also, collaborative teaching must see experience and practice as the contextual bases of knowledge. Such collaboration should challenge the split between "the sources of raw data" and "the place of academic theorizing". It must present Africans as active subjects, resistors, and creators, not just victims of their own histories and experiences. But such collaborative teaching will attest to the power of identity and its connection to knowledge production. Thus, who is teaching about Africa is equally important. In our teaching academies, physical representation of different African bodies is significant to rupturing genuine academic knowledge of Africa. Of course, this approach to teaching does not intend to be a panacea but an important step in new ways of seeing, learning, and doing.

2.5 Telling Success Stories

In my mind I think Africa is one of the few places that can be infantilized and denigrated freely without consequences or due regard to local peoples' sensitivities. Africa is a "basket case"! One only needs to watch current news media to see the voyeurism, infantilization, and degradation of the continent. Rather than focusing on the positives – the emergence of ICT-facilitated distance learning, HIV/AIDS awareness, and environmentally sustainable resource extraction and management – popular culture prefers civil wars, death, and squalor. The word *crisis* is synonymous with Africa. The Continent is all too often presented as an exercise in failures! Africa is about mal-development and failed leadership. Where are the success stories that can lift the spirit of the learner beyond the doom and gloom? Hearing so much about HIV/AIDS in Africa, one might conclude all must be dead on the continent by now. Although Africa faces many challenges, including the enormous toll of HIV/AIDS, civil unrest, and poverty, it is not all about disasters and failures. When it comes to "development" how and where do we speak about responsibilities and complicities (see also Kankwenda 1994; Ragwanja 1997; Chabal 1996). Teaching should tell the success stories as well as the failures and disasters. Learners must be exposed to successful stories about the continent that embolden the human spirit. There is an indomitable African spirit that needs unearthing in order to demonstrate the capacity of the continent to lift itself from terminal collapse. Therefore, education must challenge the "failures" of the continent. We must ask: What can we learn from the success cases? We need to consider the sites and sources of local peoples resisting and empowering themselves through their own creativity and resourcefulness. How can we devote our research and teaching focus to the African success stories as another educational strategy? There is much to be learned from the successes. How can these lessons be repeated? What are the implications of these success stories in the search for general solutions to human problems? While local communities adapt to contemporary global changes, they are also resisting the encroachment of the negative effects of globalization. There is revitalization of Indigenous cultures and cultural knowledges. This is the reclamation of relevant past cultural values in a bid to find and offer positive (solution-oriented) approaches to dealing with contemporary African problems. Arguably, and notwithstanding any good intentions, the focus on failures serves to justify the continued imperial gaze on Africa. It highlights the benevolence of those who want to "help" in the midst of disasters, crises, and destruction. Why spend time, energy, and effort determining who is responsible, complicit, and accountable for failures when there is so much disaster and crisis demanding immediate attention? The work of the imperial saviour is not about asking tough questions. It is about getting things done for the common good! The lessons of history are irrelevant in the face of facts presented to us about human disasters and the imperatives for quick action. Focusing on successes can give a feeling of complacency that things are alright. Students of Africa should know about how local peoples are surviving against the odds. We should learn about the extent of local creativity and resourcefulness in the face of human and natural disasters as well as the impact of the globalization of local, regional, and national economies.

2.6 The Dangers, Perils, and Seduction of Romanticism, Overmythicization, and the Claim to Authenticity

It is easy to romanticize Africa after so much negativity and selective misrepresentations of the continent. But critical teaching and learning must avoid this intellectual practice. It is important to be aware of the dangers of romanticization and over-mythicization as we speak and write about Africa. We also need to be attentive to how its peoples counter the negativity and untruths about the continent.

On a related point, I see all knowledges as contested. There is always a selective representation of the past and knowledge (Briggs 1996; Clifford 1983; Keesing 1989; Makang 1997; Linnekin 1991, 1992). Teaching is contested educational practice. I view with deep suspicion any claim to "authenticity" as possessing authority or authoritative voice that is not open to challenge or critique (Handler 1988). The past is itself subject to colonial and imperial contamination. But in taking this critical stance to "authenticity", I do not dismiss the power of imaginary mythologies as part of the decolonizing project. As an anti-colonial pedagogue I share Lattas' (1993: 254) view that the past must be recreated "as a way of formulating an uncolonized space to inhabit".

Claims of authenticity that serve to make dubious distinctions about who is a true "African" or not can be hollow, especially when there are no critical questions of responsibility and accountability. What are the responsibilities that come with a right to claim Africa or African "membership"? How does history complicate claims of the authentic? What do we make of the Diasporic ruptures, interruptions, continuities, and discontinuities? These questions have no easy answers except that they serve to remind us of the limits of knowing Africa. When coupled with over-mythicization, often a troubling by-product of biased media coverage, African claims of authenticity can be detrimental to the collective struggles of African peoples and their shared responsibilities to concerns and causes.

2.7 *The Socio-political Contexts of Knowledge Production*

Every space is political and contested. And, as already alluded to, so is knowledge – its production, interrogation, validation, dissemination, and application. The uses of knowledge are varied, complex, and complicated. For those of us who teach, research, write, and, in fact, "produce knowledge" about Africa, in teaching Africa it is useful to know and remember that the sources and uses of data are not apolitical. There are always profound social and political contexts and consequences for our constructions and applications of knowledge. All knowledges are contingent in particular social and political contexts. Therefore, in our teaching practices we must always be conscious of the socio-environmental and political contexts of data gathering and knowledge production. In Africa, and in most parts of our world, our people's freedoms have been taken away as they teach critically and politically.

Creating spaces for critical cutting-edge teaching and learning raise hard questions about power and leadership. It is unsatisfying when learners feel some disconnect from each other, unable to link the obligations of knowledge production to the responsibilities of scholarship to local communities. I believe academic scholarship must be pursued with rigor, openness, reflection, and self-criticality. Scholarship must be supported by research. Research must also support teaching. The responsibilities of knowledge, in my experience, lead me to shun any attempts to divorce scholarship from considerations of politics. I do not crave this separation. As a racial minority faculty in the Western academy I have come to find such separation is an unaffordable luxury. Nonetheless, I respect those who pursue the separation of scholarship and politics. It is their intellectual right and privilege. However, I consider it intellectual arrogance of the highest order when those who support this separation claim that those who think otherwise are not pursuing "true" or "real" scholarship.

Broaching both intellectual and political projects, I am not proscribing a particular "politics" as more legitimate than the other. What I am calling for is a space for the political to be meaningfully engaged as part of academic scholarship no matter how we each define the "political". If we admit that knowledge is always political and heavily contested, then what we choose to do or not do as intellectuals and researchers is a political decision and choice. When there exists an intellectual hypocrisy that masks, denigrates, and stifles the pursuit of scholarship as "advancement of knowledge to further the cause of the social", the cause of teaching critically is not served. The culture of learning must itself promote such debate over scholarship, politics, and applications of knowledge.

In concluding this chapter, I reiterate the critical questions educators and students of Africa must confront: What is your understanding of "Africa today"? What do you understand about "Teaching Africa"? What are some of the possibilities and pitfalls in teaching Africa? What are some of the major curriculum issues in teaching about Africa? How would you describe the future challenges confronting Africa? What are the responsibilities of educators and learners? What are the responsibilities of families, communities, and Elders? How do we see the link between education and democracy in Africa? How do we see the link between education and democratic participation in the African context? How would we describe the impact of globalization on African schooling and education? What is the role of education, if any, in the formulation of national identity in the African context? What is the role of education, if any, in the formulation of political ideology in the African context? What is the role of education, if any, in the resolution of conflict in the African context? What is the role of education, if any, in the search for peace, cooperation, and social justice in the African context? How do we teach about gender/gender difference in the African context? How do we teach about ethnicity/ethnic difference in the African context? How do we teach about social class/class differences in the African context? How do we teach about language/linguistic differences in the African context? How do we teach about religion/religious differences in the African contexts? How do we teach about sexuality/sexual differences in the African contexts? How do you teach about health and the environment in the African contexts? What constitutes an "African-centred" perspective? What do you see as the place of Indigenous knowledge in teaching about Africa?

These questions are, and can be informed by, the prism of an African-centred knowledge base and educational practice. This prism refers to the creation and use of African ways of knowing and seeing. By utilizing an anti-colonial discursive pedagogy – the theorization of colonial and re-colonial relations and the implications of imperial structures on knowledge production and use, the understanding of Indigenity, and the pursuit of agency, resistance, and subjective politics – we can come to a full appreciation of African-centred teaching and learning. I use "colonial" not in the conventional sense of "foreign" and "alien" but as "imposed and dominating". This view of "colonial" allows us to see how colonialism is domesticated – how those who have been oppressed by dominant discourses may find it difficult to step out of these or even to resist. Critically teaching, as part of the process of decolonization, must not simply deconstruct or question imperial, colonial, and oppressive knowledges but also subvert these cultural, symbolic, and political practices and significations (Wilson-Tagoe 1997). If anything, I see the project of this book as one conceived in the political and academic practices of imagining and creating shifting representations of knowledge that counter static and fixed definitions and interpretations of Africa.

While not having definitive answers to these questions, this book intends to contribute to the larger debate about inclusive, diverse, and equitable teaching and learning. Teaching Africa goes beyond difference to a negotiation of the self in relation to historically silenced and marginalized ways of being. In bringing these approaches to the classroom, we are empowering our students and teachers. Chapter 1 provides a theoretical Overview of how history has been – and continued to be – used as a tool of colonialism. Chapter 2 ruptures colonial history by offering a sample of African-centred data and lesson ideas for teachers. Chapter 3 provides a theoretical basis for our work by linking African-centred teaching to integrative theory. Chapter 4 extends this discussion by providing theoretical explanations of the salience of African-centred teaching and learning. Chapter 5, in connecting the central concepts of development to decolonization, provides an epistemic basis for the teaching of Africa as an educational and political project. Chapter 6 offers strategies for the reclaiming of African knowledge. Chapter 7 presents a selection of pedagogical ideas for African-centred teaching and learning. Chapter 8 cites existing African-centred models as guides for envisioning an inclusive politics of learning. Chapter 9 concludes by linking the discussion to larger sociocultural forces guiding the advocacy for and emergence of African-centred schooling: development discourses and sample lesson plans for timely and equitable studies of such issues as community empowerment, HIV/AIDS awareness, and sustainability. Timely and engaging lesson ideas and resources appear throughout the text. I invite teachers to copy these materials, develop their own, and, in the spirit of community, share their best teaching and learning practices with colleagues. Taken together, these chapters seek to offer theoretical and practical foundations from which to construct truly equitable and engaging spaces for learning. Our children need these spaces for their own growth, creative exploration, and awareness raising. I look forward to being a part of these educational journeys with you and with the students you teach.

References

Briggs, C. L. (1996) The Politics of Discursive Authority in Research on the "Invention of Tradition". *Cultural Anthropology*, 11(4), 435–469.

Chabal, P. (1996) The African Crisis: Context and Interpretation. In Werbner, R. and Ranger, T. (Eds.) *Postcolonial Identities in Africa* (pp. 29–54). London: Zed Books.

Clifford, J. (1983) On Ethnographic Authority. *Representations*, 1, 118–146.

Dei, G. J. S. (2000) Rethinking the Role of Indigenous Knowledges in the Academy. *International Journal of Inclusive Education*, 4(2), 111–132.

Dei, G. J. S. (2003) Recreating Knowledge to Teach and Learn About Africa. *Journal of Postcolonial Education*, 2(1), 39–48.

Dei, G. J. S., Hall, B. and Goldin Rosenberg, D. (2000) *Indigenous Knowledges in Global Contexts: Multiple Readings of Our World*. Toronto: University of Toronto Press.

Fanon, F. (1968) *The Wretched of the Earth*. Tr. Constance Farrington. New York: Grove.

Handler, R. (1986) Authenticity. *Anthropology Today*, 2(1), 2–4.

Kankwenda, M. (1994) 'Marabouts' and Merchants of Development in Africa. *CODESRIA Bulletin*, 3, 9–15.

Kessing, M. (1989) Creating the Past: Custom and Identity in the Contemporary Pacific. *Contemporary Pacific*, 1(1/2), 19–42.

Lattas, A. (1993) Essentialism, Memory and Resistance: Aboriginality and the Politics of Authenticity. *Oceania*, 63, 2–67.

Linnekin, J. (1991) Texts Bites and the R-Word: The Politics of Representing Scholarship. *The Contemporary Pacific*. Spring 1991, 171–176.

Linnekin, J. (1992) On The Theory and Politics of Cultural Construction in the Pacific. *Oceania*, 62, 249–263.

Makang, J. M. (1997) Of the Good Use of Tradition: Keeping the Critical Perspective in African Philosophy. In Eze, E. C. (Ed.) *Postcolonial African Philosophy: A Critical Reader* (pp. 324–338). Cambridge, MA: Blackwell Publishers.

Ragwanja, P. M. (1997) Post-Industrialism and Knowledge Production: African Intellectuals in the New International Division Labour. *CODESRIA Bulletin*, 3, 5–11.

Roberts, H. (1998). Indignous Knowledges and Western Science: Perspectives from the Pacific. In. D. Hodson (Ed.), *Science and technology Education and Ethnicity: An Aotearoa/New Zealand Perspective*. Proceedings of a conference held at the Royal Society of New Zealand, Thorndon, Wellington, May 7–8, 1996.

Semali, L. and Kincheloe, J. (eds.) (1999) *What is Indigenous Knowledge? Voices From the Academy*. New York: Falmer Press.

Sklar, R. L. (1993) The African Frontier for Political Science. In R. Bates, et al. (Eds.) *Africa and the Disciplines* (pp. 83–112). Chicago: University of Chicago Press.

Smith, L. (1999) *Decolonizing Methodologies*. London: Zed Books.

Wilson-Tagoe, N. (1997) Reading Towards a Theorization of African Women's Writing: African Women Writers with Feminist Gynocriticism. In S. Newell (Ed.) *Writing African Women: Gender, Popular Culture and Literature in West Africa* (pp. 11–28). London: Zed Books.

Yankah, K. (2004) *Globalization and the African Scholar*. Faculty of Arts University of Ghana [Monograph].

Chapter 1
History as Tool of Colonialism

Abstract In making the case that teaching African history and knowledge systems is critical for emancipatory and equitable learning, the discussion considers some of the challenges associated with this work. Specifically, the use of oral histories and biased curriculum presents obstacles for educations. These challenges can be overcome via critical engagement of texts. The chapter models teaching and learning strategies for this engagement.

Keywords Teaching · Africa · Oral history · Bias · Curriculum · Identity · Resistance · Questioning · Critical education · Learning strategies

1.1 Introduction

I begin this book with a look at history. Specifically, the chapter will introduce the student of Africa to the "uphill" challenge of telling the history of marginalized peoples in general and of African peoples specifically. For some time now, there has been an erasure of African achievements and knowledge. This erasure is by no means accidental. The discussion briefly explores the relationship between history and power, analysing the way our understandings of the past affect our understandings and experiences of the present and future. From bias and omissions in textbooks, maps, and literature to full on lies told about African peoples, this chapter will analyse the way history works as a tool that often privileges some and punishes others. For the better part of the last 500 years, Europe has been telling the story of Africa, and it has been doing so from a Eurocentric perspective. Through colonialism, Africans have been taught about themselves through a kind of European translation of their own history and geography. If you grow up in Ghana, for example, as I did, you are more likely to learn about Niagara Falls than about the river running near your town. Wherever Eurocentric education exists, be it North America, Africa, Asia, or Europe, the European invaders of Africa are celebrated while the Africans who stood up and resisted, or who were murdered in one of many genocides, are forgotten or pushed to the outskirts of dominant history. All too often, as we show in a later chapter, this practice has continued in Canada and the United States, not only with the distortion of the history of Africa but also with the history of African Canadians. The same holds true in the United States, with the history of African Americans. History is sort of battleground where today we struggle over the past to establish the terms of the future.

It is important to spend some time discussing African historiography. History is understood not simply as a story of the past. History is about the totality of a people's lived experience. History encompasses issues of culture, economics, politics, development, and spirituality. It offers cornerstones for discussing a peoples' struggles, challenges, failures, achievements, successes, and triumphs. History invokes the present and the future, providing ways to understand and imagine Africa and the African experience. We need to evoke a continual stance on history that allows us to reclaim the past, reflect on the present, and contest the future. A discussion of African historiography introduces the learner to the way history and the telling of history works, as far the connection of history to politics, power, and culture. It is important for us to engage the omissions, denials, and celebrations of the power of centrism, and the marginalization of Africa and African experiences. This is critical to examining the idea that all history is written from a particular standpoint and intellectual politics. The learner must question any history they are confronted with. The idea of education as oppressive is also critical for understanding the way power works in all contexts. Understanding history as a tool of colonialism is to look at the way history has been used by colonizers as a tool of oppression against the colonized.

If we think of history as a story or as a narrative, historiography is the creation of that story. When creating history, historians rely on a number of different sources and tools. For most of human history, people's important stories, including major events and religious myths, have passed from one generation to the next through oral histories. Although the trend, particularly in Western countries, over the last few hundred years has been towards written histories in either books, online, or elsewhere, oral histories remain an important part of most Indigenous cultures in Africa and around the world. In addition to written and oral histories, historians also use archaeological evidence, anthropology, linguistics, and scientific findings to create history. Historians use all of these tools and approaches to create new versions of history. It is this creation of history that has been called historiography. Each tool and approach to history brings its own challenges and strengths.

1.1.1 Oral History and Learning and Teaching Africa

Oral history is the oldest form of historiography. It has happened in every society since the beginning of human communication. Oral history is the telling and passing on of important stories from one generation to the next through speech or music. In every family, community, and society there are important stories which help our understanding of each other and ourselves. These stories explain where we come from and help us to understand where we are as well as where we are going. Many cultures tell a creation story, explaining the origin of a community, a people, or of humankind. On a smaller scale, oral histories help us to navigate the history of our own families. As you know, certain stories are the "key" stories of one's family history. These may include the story of one's family's immigration to Canada or the Americas, last year or 100 years ago. These may include the story of one's parents' marriage or separation. These may include the achievements of a grandmother who anchors the family, the tragedy of a deceased parent, uncle, or sibling, or the experiences of a parent or caregiver who confronted challenges. Oral histories may also tell the story of a people's struggle against oppression. During slavery in the United States and Canada, for example, many enslaved people, most of whom were forbidden to read for fear of insurrection, used oral histories to educate their children and brethren about African religion and culture. They tried to preserve the connection to a land from which they had been so brutally stolen. Oral history is not just talk. Cultures relying on oral transmission of history and religion need specially selected individuals to carry and pass on that knowledge. These are caretakers of knowledge who perform a similar task, keeping watch over a particular history. In many cultures, only these custodians of knowledge are permitted to pass it on. Many Indigenous groups in Africa and North America used this system to protect their culture and histories from invading Europeans who sought to exterminate their culture and histories. A continuing challenge comes in figuring out how to teach histories that have traditionally been oral in mainstream schools in North America. Many Indigenous cultures do not want their histories told by academics in textbooks. At the same time, many of these same groups recognize the need to get away from the Eurocentricity which characterizes history education across the country. Investigating the histories and achievements of all of the people calling this land home provides opportunities for these voices and stories to be heard.

1.1.2 Learning and Teaching Africa Through Written History

Although spoken language and drawings came before writing, written history is now by far the most common expression of historiography. The first written alphabet was found in Egypt, over 2,500 years before the birth of Mohammad, and 3,000 years before the birth of Christ. Following the Africans, Greek and Roman peoples took up the writing of history. For centuries following the time of Mohammad (5700 A.D.), African and Islamic scholars across Northern, Central, and Southern Africa and the Middle East documented the cultural and religious ideas of their time. Beginning at the same time, written communication was also widespread in Indigenous communities throughout South, Central, and North America. Over the last 500 years, European peoples and ideas have dominated written history. As we discuss later when Europe expanded its power and influence around the world, the writing of history – the history of European "explorers" as well as the history of the Indigenous people being invaded – was an important tool used by the colonizers in their attempts at conquest. Like oral history, written history also has its caretakers and custodians. Teachers, professors, and authors all either create or work with written histories. Written history took on a new significance when employed by the Europeans in their colonial projects. This transformation may not prove nearly as significant as the change unfolding in our lifetime: the Internet and its revolutionizing of history and historiography. Although most people do not yet have access to the Internet, most of the information that can be stored electronically can easily be shared. The entire body of human writing may well be saved in electronic format in your lifetime. It is difficult to understand the implications this will have for the way we understand history.

1.1.3 Learning and Teaching Africa: Archaeological Evidence, Anthropology, Linguistics, and Science

Sometimes no oral history exists to tell the story of a people or a culture. For example, when a people like Newfoundland's Beothuks were rendered extinct through European genocide, no one was left to tell their stories. Other times, no written history exists to tell the story of a civilization. In the absence of written or oral history, historians are forced to look to other sources for information. Archaeological evidence provides important information about a number of different elements of societies for which no formal history has been passed down through writing or telling. Archaeological findings of cities, buildings, graves, pottery, important religious locations, and public gathering sites provide information on almost all aspects of a society: its technology, social relations, health and life expectancy, eating habits, and living patterns. All forms of historical evidence require interpretation. Archaeological interpretation comes with a particular set of challenges. It requires a number of highly skilled experts to determine what an item is, the era it is from, and how it may have been used. Further, there is often dispute about all of these things among the experts themselves. Anthropology can assist historians by analysing contemporary cultures, groups, and societies to see what can be learned about their past. Linguistics, the study of human speech and language, as well as the development and modification thereof, can also assist historians in piecing together information about groups, cultures, and societies from the past. Language can sometimes serve as a time capsule, connecting us to the people and cultures of the past. Although history, anthropology, and linguistics are referred to as social sciences, the word *science* usually refers to the natural sciences like Biology, Chemistry, and Geology. These fields can also be helpful to historians as they can often reveal information about the human body, the earth's environment, climatic factors, and other very important information about the past.

1.2 History and Its Connection to Politics, Culture, and Power

Although oral history, written history, and archaeology differ greatly in many ways, they share a common element as far as historiography: they all involve and require interpretation and reading between the lines. To create history, historians have to assemble these sources into a story. This means that historians have a number of difficult and important decisions to make: (1) what the sources mean; (2) whether or not the sources are accurate; (3) which sources should be left out and which should be included; and (4) how to weave together the sources to make a clear and understandable narrative. Let us think of the past as a storybook, the pages of which have been ripped up and thrown into the air. Historians pick up as many pieces as possible and put the story back together. The problem is that there is no way to know the real – or the original – story. Since some pieces are missing, there is no way to know the original order of the words. So, part of the job of the historian is to fill in the blanks and read between the lines.

When researching Ancient Rome, for example, Michael Parenti (2003) found that among the thousands of historical books, movies, and other resources on Rome, almost none of them told the story of the Roman poor, Rome's enslaved population, or Rome's women. Even among a huge collection of resources, he found there were some pretty huge missing pieces. Parenti was forced to read against the grain of mainstream Roman history, listening for silences and omissions, and make informed assumptions about the people left out of official Roman history. In his book, *The Assassination of Julius Caesar: A People's History of the Roman Republic*, Parenti attempts to make new history out of the old sources while interrogating these sources. Parenti looked into the lifestyles of some of the most important authors of Roman history. He found out that the authors, notably those who omitted the poor, women, and the enslaved when writing history, tended to be rich white men. "The writing of history has long been a privileged calling undertaken within the church, royal court, landed estate, affluent town house, government agency, university and corporate funded foundation" (Parenti 2003: 13). In this passage, Parenti is saying that the rich and powerful have been the writers of history and that this has led to history being almost entirely focused on the rich and the powerful. As a result, most people studying Ancient Rome learn only the stories, perspectives, and achievements of wealthy and powerful Romans. This pattern is by no means unique to Rome and Roman history. What have you learned about women and poor people in Canadian and European history?

It is when historians get into the muddy waters of interpreting sources, reading between the lines, and filling in the blanks that their biases, politics, and opinions come out. All history is written from particular perspectives and intellectual politics. There is no such thing as a totally objective historical account because all history is subjective. This is not to say that there is necessarily something wrong with historians working from a particular position or perspective. For example, Michael Parenti's book was written in an attempt to represent the perspectives and realities of poor, working class, and enslaved Romans. This book is written from an African-centred perspective. In the succeeding chapters, this perspective will become clear to the reader. This is so that the reader knows where the author is coming from and why. Problems arise when historians assume, or claim, that the history they are writing or presenting is totally objective, free of the politics, perspectives, and opinions of the historian. Unfortunately, many historians and history books make precisely these claims to objectivity. In order to give you the tools to read between the lines of the texts you are given in school and elsewhere, the next section of this chapter identifies a number of approaches for reading against the grain and identifying the politics, opinions, and perspectives behind whatever you are reading.

It is important for teaching and learning about Africa for us to read critically about the omissions and negations while understanding why we celebrate Africa, its peoples, and their histories. It is also significant for readers to know why we need to centre the African experience in youth education to appreciate the historic resistance and struggles of African peoples to global oppression and marginalization of identities and experiences. The question then is: why are knowing and celebrating African history important? History is important for many lessons. African history, like all history, is not just for people of African descent. It is a history of humanity. We have a collective responsibility to know the importance of that history. African history is replete with struggles, resistance, failures, and successes. A community cannot free itself from the shackles of its past and the implications of history. History should not be about forgetting. It should be about remembering not to repeat mistakes of the past. But history must be told in a way that offers hope and vision of a future for people. Given that the past is still with us today, we must speak of the past, our achievements, and contributions, while contesting any injustices and the future prospects for justice and equity. As a celebration for all of humanity, African history teaches the momentous task that all peoples must be able to tell their own histories in the fight for social justice.

There are three main reasons for advancing the cause of African history in teaching and learning about Africa. First, we must reclaim and affirm our past intellectual traditions, knowledge, and contributions to world history as a necessary exercise in our decolonization. We, as African and African diasporic people, have rich traditions of history, culture, and knowledge. All learners should be told about the complete history of ideas and events that continue to shape human growth and development. It is a primary exercise in intellectual decolonization for the oppressed to think through their own/home-grown solutions to problems. Second, we should view such history as the basis to understand the past, reflect on the present, and to project and contest the future. African history offers the basis for all peoples of African descent to search for and create a new vision for the future. The lessons of successes and failures in the past must illuminate contemporary struggles and help foster creative projects for the future. Third, history is about the search for unity of purpose among diverse groups. Thus it is necessary to theorize Africa beyond its geographical boundaries. In other words, it is important to understand the nature and complexity of the problems and challenges facing us as a people today, especially education, health, and development, and how a critical reflection is required to develop a collective consciousness of our shared realities and interdependent social existence. Teaching and learning African history offer time to strategize and rethink ways of collectively moving forward as communities. Today, there is the unilateral fragmentation around difference and the disturbing propensity of dominant groups to conscript the idea of a "fractured community" in order to deny responsibility and accountability. Developing a collective consciousness is only possible if we heal ourselves as a people – spiritually, mentally, and materially. This calls for an affirmation of the African sense of community, social responsibility, and spiritual re-embodiment.

Students can begin to learn about the important contributions that peoples of African descent have and continue to make to strengthen our various communities, to learn about the success cases, and to challenge the negative stereotypes that continue to be perpetuated on African/Black communities. Like any community, the Black and African community is diverse: there are differences in ethnicity, gender, geography, class, sexuality, language, age, and ability. We do not all think alike, nor should we. It is acceptable for members of a community to hold different agendas and opinions. This diversity does not detract from the existence of a *community*. African history calls on all of us to acknowledge the "unity in sameness" as well as the "unity in diversity". It is a time for us to reward rather than punish resistance struggles geared to bring about healthy changes in our communities. It calls us to speak out clearly and boldly about wrongs of society and to recognize silence in the midst of oppression. Failure to speak out makes one complicit to oppression.

Teaching about Africa intensifies the search for a new anti-colonial actionable politics that allows the "Black and African struggles" to continue the struggle for justice, recognition, and development. African history is bigger even than Africa. In fact, the success of the African people's liberation and empowerment will depend on the ability to connect the struggles for race, sexual, class, gender politics, Indigenous peoples' rights, and shared global environmental and health concerns. This means joining in the struggles of African and other oppressed peoples throughout the world. The causes of African history would be about broader politics and collective social vision.

It is important for contemporary learners to interrogate the world around us. Advertisements on the bus, textbooks from your school, newspapers (the sports section too!), stories an aunt may tell us – whoever or whatever is conveying information will have some influence over what is told. In order to make sense of all this, it is important to interrogate the information and assess where it is coming from and why. I offer a few critical analysis tools for understanding any text you may come across (a "text" can be written, spoken, performed, and presented in a host of ways). Using a sample text, we will examine the following indicators of bias, perspective, and opinion: omission, celebration, centrism, and marginalization. When we look at *omission*, we try to identify what is missing in the text – any information relating to the event, idea, or history in question which is absent from the text. When we look at *celebration*, we try to identify the events and/or people that are treated as important, worthy, good and/or relevant in the text. When we look at *centrism*, we try to identify the ideas, events and/or people at the centre of the text – usually a text focuses on particular ideas, people and/or events. When we look at *marginalization*, we try to identify the ideas, events and/or people that have been pushed to the margins of the text. Think of the margins of a regular sheet of paper – the centre is reserved for the important information while the margin is reserved for less important ideas.

After reading the following text about early Portuguese expeditions to Africa, taken from Wikipedia, we will use the ideas of omission, celebration, centrism, and marginalization to identify the writer's perspective and politics.

Portuguese Expeditions (http://en.wikipedia.org/wiki/European_exploration_of_Africa, Accessed: 10/18/2007)

> Portuguese explorer Prince Henry, known as the Navigator, was the first European to methodically explore Africa and the oceanic route to the Indies. From his residence in the Algarve region of southern Portugal, he directed successive expeditions to circumnavigate Africa and reach India. In 1420, Henry sent an expedition to secure the uninhabited but strategic island of Madeira. In 1425, he tried to secure the Canary Islands as well, but these were already under firm Castilian control. In 1431, another Portuguese expedition reached and annexed the Azores.
>
> Along the western and eastern coasts of Africa, progress was also steady; Portuguese sailors reached Cape Bojador in 1434 and Cape Blanco in 1441. In 1433, they built a fortress on the island of Arguin, in modern day Mauritania, trading European wheat and cloth for African gold and slaves. It was the first time that the semi-mythic gold of the Sudan reached Europe without Muslim mediation. Most of the slaves were sent to Madeira, which became, after thorough deforestation, the first European plantation colony. Between 1444 and 1447, the Portuguese explored the coasts of Senegal, Gambia, and Guinea. In 1456, a Venetian captain under Portuguese command explored the islands of Cape Verde. In 1462, two years after Prince Henry's death, Portuguese sailors explored the Bissau islands and named Sierra Leoa (Lion Range).
>
> In 1469, Fernão Gomes rented the rights of African exploration for five years. Under his direction, in 1471, the Portuguese reached modern Ghana and settled in La Mina (the mine), later renamed Elmina. They had finally reached a country with an abundance of gold, hence the historical name of "Gold Coast" that Elmina would eventually receive.
>
> In 1472, Fernão do Po discovered the island that would bear his name for centuries (now Bioko) and an estuary abundant in shrimp (Portuguese: camaron), giving its name to Cameroon.
>
> Soon after, the equator was crossed by Europeans. Portugal established a base in São Tomé that, after 1485, was settled with criminals. After 1497, expelled Spanish and Portuguese Jews also found a safe haven there.
>
> In 1482, Diego Cao found the mouth of a large river and learned of the existence of a great kingdom, Kongo. In 1485, he explored the river upstream as well.
>
> But the Portuguese wanted, above anything else, to find a route to India and kept trying to circumnavigate Africa. In 1485, the expedition of João Afonso d'Aveiros, with the German astronomer Martin of Behaim as part of the crew, explored the Bight of Benin, returning information about African king Ogane.
>
> In 1488, Bartholomeu Dias and his pilot Pedro d'Alemquer, after putting down a mutiny, turned a cape where they were caught by a storm, naming it Cape of Storms. They followed the coast for a while realizing that it kept going eastward with even some tendency to the north. Lacking supplies, they turned around with the conviction that the far end of Africa had finally been reached. Upon their return to Portugal the promising cape was renamed Cape of Good Hope.
>
> Some years later, Christopher Columbus landed in America under rival Castilian command. Pope Alexander VI decreed the Inter caetera bull, dividing the non-Christian parts of the world between the two rival Catholic powers, Spain and Portugal.

Omission: What is missing from this text? Although the historical story told here takes place in Africa, the experience of Africa is missing. When the Portuguese "explored" these regions, they constructed slave-trading networks that routinely involved the kidnapping, imprisonment, rape, and murder of Africa peoples. We learn of what the Portuguese had in mind, their decisions, their ideas, their aspirations, and even their challenges, but nothing as far as the ideas, decisions, or struggles of African people. Imagine telling the story of Africa without Africans. What does this erasure mean for the study of history? How best to reclaim a place for these erased histories?

Celebration: Who or what is celebrated in this text? The key people in this text are Portuguese explorers. The events celebrated are their achievements in the conquest of Africa: renaming, taking over, and displacing African peoples.

Centrism: What does this text focus on? Who or what is at the centre of this text? Similar to our findings on the issue of *celebration*, this text centres on just one thing: the success of Portuguese colonial "exploration" in Africa. This Eurocentric text tells one story at the expense of all the others. Further, it dresses up brutal violence as something acceptable, even noble.

Marginalization: What has been pushed to the side in this text? While Portuguese explorers and priorities are featured quite prominently, Africans are mentioned only twice, and both times as slaves. The second paragraph describes the trade of "African gold and slaves" as if people were just another thing the Portuguese "found" in Africa – a natural resource to be exploited like copper, tobacco, or livestock, or any other commodity.

Using the above analysis of omission, celebration, centrism, and marginalization, we learn that this text is Eurocentric. It ignores African perspectives; we do not need anyone to tell us that the Africans who encountered these explorers-as-murderers, rapists, and enslavers would tell this story a lot differently. Further, with the exception of two references to "slaves", the text implies that Africans were all but absent when the Portuguese came to Africa. This text is a product of Eurocentric historiography. Its authors have discarded the opinions, experiences, and achievements of Africans in this text. By ignoring the violence of the Portuguese against Africans, whether they meant to or not, the authors have also condoned it. Whose violence does our society allow us to forget, and whose are we forced to remember?

Although the discussion and analysis has focused on the degree to which Europeans dominate the text above, even the discussion of the Portuguese has some missing pieces. For example, who performed the challenging jobs in the day-to-day work of Portuguese colonialism? While the text mentions the achievements of Prince Henry, Fernão do Po, Diego Cao, and Bartholomeu Dias, it does not tell us who cleared the trails, who did the heavy lifting, who wrote the maps, who was sent into battle first, or who paid with their lives for Portuguese "progress". We do not learn about the Portuguese workers – those exploited by their own people. Finally we may notice that we hear nothing of the role that women played in any of these events.

1.2.1 Test: Evaluation/Assessment

In order that readers follow the African-centred perspective undertaken for this book we offer a test. After reading the historical summary of Western settlement in Canada from the *Encyclopaedia Britannica*, perform an analysis of omission, celebration, centrism, and marginalization in the text, like the one we have just completed above:

Settlement and Exploration in the West (From the encyclopedia Britannica, http://www.britannica.com/eb/article-198167/Canada, accessed: 10/18/2007)

> The Canadian prairies were not entirely unknown even in the days of New France. As early as the 1730s a family of explorers headed by Pierre Gaultier de Varennes, sieur de La Vérendrye, began a series of overland explorations far to the west of Lake Superior. Their travels carried them into what is now the western United States, perhaps as far as the foothills of the Rockies. They visited Lake Winnipeg, the Red River, the Assiniboine River, and the Saskatchewan River as far upstream as the fork formed by the North and South Saskatchewan headstreams.
>
> The posts of the Hudson's Bay Company had given England a preferred jumping-off point for exploration of the Canadian west. An expedition under Henry Kelsey explored part of that territory in 1690, long before the journeys of the La Vérendryes. In 1754 Anthony Henday traveled from Hudson Bay as far as the foothills of the Rockies, reaching a point near the site of present-day Red Deer, Alta. Another Hudson's Bay Company trader, Samuel Hearne, discovered Great Slave Lake in 1771, and by descending the Coppermine River to its mouth, he became the first European to reach the Arctic Ocean by land. Although the Rockies still barred the overland route to the western ocean, the Pacific coast of Canada was visited by sea in 1778, when Capt. James Cook explored the northwest coastline from Vancouver Island to Alaska.
>
> In 1783 a group of Montreal merchants founded the powerful North West Company. Not only did the new fur-trading company provide sharp competition, but its trappers explored large parts of the previously unknown expanses of the Canadian west. In 1789 Alexander Mackenzie (a Nor'wester, as agents of the North West Company were called) followed the river that now bears his name from its source to the Arctic Ocean.
>
> Disappointed because he had not discovered a route to the Pacific, he set out on another expedition in 1792. After a strenuous journey over the most rugged terrain on the continent, Mackenzie and his companions at last crossed the Rocky Mountains to reach the Fraser River in 1793. From the Fraser they portaged to the Bella Coola, which they descended until they sighted the long-sought western sea. Only a few weeks earlier Capt. George Vancouver had explored the same part of the Pacific coast by sea.
>
> Mackenzie's journey was the first made by a European across the continent in either Canada or the United States. In 1808 the Fraser River was thoroughly explored by Simon Fraser, after whom it is named. In 1811 David Thompson completed his exploration of the Columbia from its source, in southeastern British Columbia, to its mouth, in what is now Oregon.

Let us consider how this text could be used as a form of critical awareness in the classroom. Here is a sample lesson with a critical focus.

Lesson Title: Hearing Silenced Voices

Curriculum Expectations: Teachers will refer to the relevant curriculum expectations. This lesson may apply to History, Social Studies, Media, and English courses.

Description/Lesson Objective: Students will continue to build upon their knowledge and critical thinking skills by considering the multiple voices and stories from the past, the different stories they tell, and how some stories are heard more than others.

1.2 History and Its Connection to Politics, Culture, and Power

Materials Required: Students will be provided with a copy of *Settlement and Exploration in the West*.

Planning Notes: Teachers are invited to liaise with the local Aboriginal communities to foster strong community-classroom ties.

Accommodations:

- Collaborate with colleagues. Review with colleagues from the Special Education and Guidance Departments to determine effective and relevant strategies to support student learning.
- Pre-teach vocabulary.
- Provide copies of teacher's notes, as requested, by students.
- Provide accessible copies of handouts (e.g., large font).
- Arrange for students to have study peers.
- Provide additional time for students to write material from the board.

Equitable Teaching/Learning Activities:

- As a pre-reading activity, ask students to think about the following question: *Whose stories appear in the official account of history, often in textbooks?*
- The students share their insights in small groups and during a class discussion. Ideas are recorded on the board as part of a brainstorm. Students are asked to note these ideas.
- Teacher defines key terms on the board. Here are some suggestions:
  - *Official History*
  - *Unofficial History*
  - *Canon*
  - *Omission*
  - *Celebration (in a text)*
  - *Centrism*
  - *Marginalization*

  These terms will be added to the Word Wall.
- The teacher asks the students to relate the terms to the article *Settlement and Exploration in the West*.
- Teacher distributes copies of the article.
- In support of varied approaches to literacy, the teacher reviews effective reading practices (e.g., highlighting key ideas and new words, re-reading the article). The teacher and student volunteers read part of the article aloud or silently.
- The teacher provides the students with the following visual organizer:

Perspective of the author	Evidence from the text (quotations)
Omission (What is left out of the text?):	
Celebration (What is celebrated?):	
Centrism (What is the focus of the text?):	
Marginalization (What is not emphasized in the text?):	

- The teacher assigns each student one of the roles: as a spokesperson for omission, centrism, celebration, and marginalization.
- Working in mixed groups, and speaking from their varied perspectives, the students discuss the article. They complete the organizer.
- The students begin an extension project to identify and research the unheard voices in this historic account: those of Aboriginals. They will present their experience of Western settlement and exploration in the form of one of the following:
    ◦ Research essay
    ◦ Photo essay
    ◦ Portfolio with text and visuals
    ◦ Website
    ◦ Poster, drawing, or other visual depiction
    ◦ Dramatic presentation
    ◦ Debate (Aboriginal and non-Aboriginal perspectives of settlement and exploration)
- The teacher may wish to invite Aboriginal Elders to share their experiences with the students as part of an ongoing dialogue and relationship building between the school and the wider community.

Assessment and Evaluation Strategies:

- The teacher circulates around the classroom to listen to and provide assistance to students during the group discussion.
- The teacher may wish to collect the completed visual organizers and provide feedback to students.
- Students complete a rough draft of their work and receive assessment (feedback) from the teacher prior to submitting the final version for evaluation.

Teacher Reflections: To be completed at the end of the lesson.

1.3 Conclusion

Although this discussion so far has looked at some pretty disturbing trends, it is fair to acknowledge that the story of history is not all bad news. We know that many Africans on the Continent and in the Diaspora are revising, revisioning, and rewriting the history of the African continent as well as that of the various communities within global African Diaspora. The job is not simply to create new history but to also interrogate the histories we have been already taught – the histories which whether we know it or not – that form the basis of many of our opinions. For many of us, our knowledge and our way of seeing the world have been shaped by a Eurocentric lens. Too many of us have come to understand ourselves and our places in the world through a racist looking glass. While some of us have learned that our history is the only one that matters, others have learned that our history is of no value or worse, that it is non-existent. To return to the example of Ghana, generation after generation of Eurocentric education – marginalizing Africans and centring white people and their cultures – has created a society in which skin-whitening cream is a hugely popular product, used by people in all areas of the country. The same is true in India and dozens of countries around the world with majority non-white populations. To liberate ourselves from a Eurocentric history is to begin the process of liberating ourselves from a Eurocentric present and future.

In this chapter, hopefully readers have been given some of the tools to begin this undertaking. Ultimately, the students of Africa and the African experience will construct and design their own lenses for seeing and understanding history and the world around them. The tools outlined in this chapter will assist the reader to construct one's own lens which places multiple perspectives at its centre, which does not marginalize other people and their history, and which omits nothing and no one. History is a high stakes political game. It can fuel or fight racism, sexism, homophobia, and able-ism. It is a tool of the colonizer but can also be a tool of decolonization. We may elect to use it as a tool for liberation. The next chapter seeks to reclaim lost African history by detailing a selection of lesson topics and ideas for educators.

Reference

Parenti, M. (2003). *The Assignation of Julius Caesar: A People's History of the Roman Republic*. New York: Knopff.

Chapter 2
Teaching and Learning African History

Abstract This discussion traces some of the most salient and enduring philosophies, political premises, and thinkers underlying the contemporary African-centred movement. These are connected to contemporary efforts to realize African-centred schooling in the United States, Canada, and Europe. Highlighting a broad range of African contributions to contemporary history from the 1600s to the present day, the chapter concludes with practical strategies for engagement of students with these issues.

Keywords African history · Philosophy · African-centred schooling · African local knowledges · Curriculum design · Learning activities · Du Bois · Ontario curriculum · Curriculum expectations · Curriculum omissions

2.1 Introduction

It is fitting to bring home the ways teaching and learning about Africa and the African experience can be made more relevant to the education of youth in North America, especially to the cause of Black and minority education in Canada. We use the teaching of African history to foreground the discussion. As noted in the opening chapter, all textbooks have a reason for being, and all textbooks are written from a particular perspective. This chapter introduces a selection of the major events, achievements, and struggles of African Canadians over the past 400 years that could inform the teaching of African-Canadian history to youth in the school system. We begin by reiterating some of the ways contemporary education has been geared to teach students about Europe and Europeans, while ignoring Africa and African peoples. Mindful of the missing history of African Canadians, this chapter provides a timeline of some of the major events, achievements, and struggles of African Canadian peoples.

Eurocentricity is a way of viewing and understanding a world that places Europe at the centre of all knowledge. Eurocentricity is focused on and celebrates European peoples, history, religions, ideas, and cultures. A Eurocentric view of the world holds that European ideas and cultures are superior to all other ideas and culture, and views non-European ideas and culture as different from what is *normal*. Eurocentricity is a standard for judging everything that is NOT European. Have we ever heard the term *ethnic food*? Let us think about what food is not ethnic food, and one will begin to understand the way Canadian and American societies are Eurocentric.

In order for someone to have a Eurocentric view, he or she must be taught to think in such a way. Europe is seen as the centre of knowledge. Its values, ideas, norms, and practices reign valid and supreme. Everything else is measured against European standards. Not surprisingly, many students of European descent grow up thinking their way of life is superior to that of others, while their non-European counterparts feel theirs is lacking and must therefore strive for acceptance and achieve legitimacy in the eyes of the dominant. Our view of the world comes from a number of different places, including our family, our peers, our teachers, our schools, our religious and spiritual communities, and the media.

If we take our schools as an example, we can see some of the ways that Eurocentricity is taught. Everyday there are thousands working to educate – working to give the learner a particular outlook on life. Some are teachers, some are writing the rules for how and what you should be taught, some are writing books, and others are making decisions about who, what, and how much will go where. Some work for the government and some do not. Each one of these "educators", whether we know it or not, has an idea about what and how the learner should or ought to think. All these people go into one's school experience – the place where the learner has spent half of his or her "waking" or "working" life so far. Let us consider diversity. Identify which holidays have been taught to learners in our North American schools? What holidays are celebrated in the school? For example, name the official holidays necessitating school closures? In North America, rather tellingly, the only holidays that will get the student out of school are Christmas, Thanksgiving, Easter, and national holidays like Independence Day and Canada Day. In accordance with the *Charter of Rights and Freedoms*, public schools accommodate students celebrating religious holidays by providing time away from classes without academic penalty. Beyond holidays, if the school has a cafeteria, what sort of food does it serve? Does it have kosher of halal options? Does the cafeteria serve what someone with a Eurocentric mindset would call ethnic food, or does it serve what that person would call regular food? Where do the sports come from that are taught in gym? In the hallways and classrooms, whose faces and ideas are represented on the pictures and slogans on the walls? In our textbooks, whose histories do we learn? Whose achievements are discussed in our classes? In most North American schools, European peoples, ideas, and culture are the foci in almost all areas of learning. This is no accident. Although our teachers, vice-principals and principals have not exactly conspired to hide away African, Asian, Aboriginal/First Nations, and Latin American histories and perspectives, it is no accident that these histories are missing from our education. In many cases, African, Asian, Aboriginal/First Nations, and Latin American peoples and histories are missing from the curriculum.

2.1 Introduction

In Ontario, home to over 700,000 students and 850 public schools, also the most populous and ethno-racially diverse province in Canada, there is a growing awareness, policy development, and implementation of equitable teaching and learning practices and curriculum content. The recent *Equity and Inclusive Education Strategy* (Ontario 2009) announced by the Ontario Ministry of Education expands upon the existing *Antiracism and Ethnocultural Equity in School Boards: Guidelines for Policy Development and Implementation* (Ontario 1993). The recent policy development recognizes the existence of and barriers created by such social oppressions as racism, sexism, homophobia, ableism, and other forms of discrimination. Part of the province-wide Student Success Strategy, this increased focus on equity centres on supporting students' self-esteem while creating conditions for their achievement. Some positive steps, including the use of differentiated instruction – using various instructional strategies to engage students and to respond to their strengths, including visual, auditory, kinaesthetic styles – and a more diversified curriculum are advocated; however, the systemic dismantling of oppressions, not surprisingly, is beyond the scope of this current policy iteration.

Looking at the curriculum, the equity-driven changes are happening slowly. The only Canadian History course students have to take in high school is *Canadian History Since World War I*, a course students usually take in the tenth grade. A look at the curriculum reveals that one learning expectation makes reference to Black Canadians and one makes reference to Africa – the latter referring to the AIDS crisis (Ontario Ministry of Education and Training 2005a,b).

Encouragingly, a fairly recent addition to the Ontario curriculum offers the promise of a more diversified learning experience. *The History of Africa and Peoples of African Descent*, a grade 11 open course, traces the history of African peoples from ancient times to the current era. This ambitious survey course, an elective course with the prerequisite of successful completion of *Canadian History Since World War I*, is gaining in popularity and is well-received by students. Not intended as an African-centred course in the pure philosophical sense, the course expands students' awareness of and engagement with Africa.

For example, the entire English curriculum for grades 9, 10, and 12 in Ontario, to cite one example reflecting current practices, does not mandate the study of Black or African people, writers, or scholars, but does afford teachers the professional discretion to select works by diverse authors (Ontario Ministry of Education and Training 1999, 2003). The history of African Canadians and the accomplishments of Africans are missing. In Ontario, the learning expectations for grade 12 philosophy make over forty-five references to philosophers. Only 5 of these are to non-Europeans, and none are to African thinkers (Public District School Board Writing Partnership 2002). The Classical Civilization (grade 12) course ignores Africans altogether (Ontario 2000a). The course focuses entirely on ancient Greece and Rome, ignoring African, Asian, Latin American, and Indigenous societies as a whole. Let us remember that these courses are not called "European Philosophy" or "European Ancient Civilizations". By ignoring the ideas and cultures of African, Asian, Latin American, and Indigenous peoples, the curriculum sends a message that these ideas, histories, and cultures are not worth talking about. As a result, a student is being taught that European ideas and culture will provide you with the necessary tools to understand and succeed in this world – the dominant world. For many students, this Eurocentric education serves to amputate them from their pasts. This is the Eurocentric approach to understanding the world and its history. However, opportunities to consider African history and experiences abound in a wide range of Geography and History courses in Ontario:

Geography:

- Physical Geography: Patterns, Processes, and Interactions, Grade 11, University/College Preparation (CGF3M)
- Geographics: The Geographer's Toolkit, Grade 11, Workplace Preparation (CGT3E)
- Travel and Tourism: A Regional Geographic Perspective, Grade 11, Open (CGG3O)
- Canadian and World Issues: A Geographic Analysis, Grade 12, University Preparation (CGW4U)
- World Geography: Human Patterns and Interactions, Grade 12, University Preparation (CGU4U)
- World Geography: Urban Patterns and Interactions, Grade 12, College Preparation (CGU4C)

History:

- World History to the Sixteenth Century, Grade 11, University/College Preparation (CHW3M)
- World History Since 1900: Global and Regional Perspectives, Grade 11, Open (CHT3O)
- World History: The West and the World, Grade 12, University Preparation (CHY4U)
- World History: The West and the World, Grade 12, College Preparation (CHY4C)
- Adventures in World History, Grade 12, Workplace Preparation (CHM4E)

Since Canada and the United States were originally the offspring of Europe, it would be natural to focus on European history, culture, and people. Let us rethink that for a second. Who are the founding peoples of Canada and the United States? With Indigenous peoples being the founding nations, how does one find a place when we already have people living there? The learner may have been taught that the French and British alone established a colony and a civilization on the territory we now call Canada. Similarly, the prevailing story of the 1492 conquest of the Americas, but one that is increasingly challenged, centres Europeans experiences while silencing the Indigenous peoples in South, Central, and North America and the Caribbean. What many people do not know is that alongside the British and the French, Africans are also Canada's "founding people". It is important to know that the British and French are inextricably tied to Africa and African people by colonialism and neocolonialism. The learner cannot forget the Indigenous people of this part of the world, who record their civilization all the way back to what they see as the beginning of time. Finally, Canada is one of the most multicultural countries in the world. Canada now has its roots in every corner of the globe. So, as we record and tell the story of our history, a Eurocentric approach simply does not work.

2.2 Making the Case for African-Centred Education: The Roots and Place of African-Centredity

African-centredity is a theory for social change that aims to improve the lives of African people around the world. With one of their first references appearing in 1980, the terms *African-centredity* and *African-centred* were coined by Molefi Kete Asante, an African American professor (Asante 2003, originally published in 1980). One of the main ideas at the core of African-centredity is that in order to understand and prepare for our future, we must understand our past. This book views history as a central point of discussion, one that can help with the task of connecting the present and the future by understanding some important things about the past. According to Asante, African-centredity is defined as:

> a mode of thought and action in which the centrality of African interests, values, and perspectives predominate. In regards to theory, it is the placing of African people in the centre of any analysis of African phenomena. Thus, it is possible for anyone to master the discipline of seeking the location of Africans in a given phenomenon. In terms of action and behaviour, it is a devotion to the idea that what is in the best interest of African consciousness is at the heart of ethical behaviour. Finally, African-centredity seeks to enshrine the idea that blackness itself is a trope of ethics. Thus, to be Black is to be against all forms of oppression, racism, classism, homophobia, patriarchy, child abuse, pedophilia, and white racial domination (Asante 2003: 2).

In telling the story – the processes of teaching and learning about Africa – we must all bear these ideas in mind. African peoples, ideas, and approaches to history should be at the centre of teaching and learning about Black experiences. If we look at textbooks schools have used in the past or even continue to use today we can ask some critical questions: Whose ideas are at the centre of these books? Whose stories did these books tell? Where did the ideas in these books come from? We cannot forget about our math and science texts – whose discoveries do these books celebrate? Did they give examples that reflected all histories and all peoples or only one's histories? How about the histories and heritage of others in our classes? Who and what has been left out of the books the school has asked students to read?

As early as the beginning of the twentieth century, African American and Caribbean scholars, activists, and popular intellectuals argued that even though slavery had been abolished, Africans in the Diaspora still faced extreme discrimination. Many of these pioneers thought it was important to build an awareness among African peoples of the way racism works in order to resist the white supremacy facing Africans in the Diaspora. W.E.B. Du Bois was an African American scholar, poet, and activist. He was the first African American to earn and receive a doctorate from Harvard University. He was also one of the first Americans to theorize the race problem in the United States. To this day, he remains one of the central inspirations for African-centredity. Du Bois co-founded the National Association for the Advancement of Colored People (NAACP) and was the editor-in-chief of the NAACP's magazine, *The Crisis: A Record of the Darker Races*. Although terms like "Coloured People" and "Darker Races" sound outdated and racist today, at the time they were a lot better than the words many whites used to refer to Africans and African Americans. Du Bois thought that Africans needed to understand race differently in order to resist and overcome the inequality facing them. He devoted his life to helping his fellow Africans with this very task. Du Bois' understanding of race inspired countless Americans of all colours, and he is widely remembered as the founder of the modern civil rights movement in the United States.

Although they had different ideas on how best to fight against the racism and oppression facing Africans on the continent and the Diaspora, Marcus Mosiah Garvey was another key inspiration for African-centredity. Garvey founded the Universal Negro Improvement Association and African Communities League (UNIL-ACL), a worldwide organization. Garvey and the UNIL-ACL campaigned for the Back-to-Africa movement, arguing that Africans in the Diaspora needed to return to Africa in order to escape the difficult lives and living conditions of Africans in the Diaspora and on the continent. By 1920, the UNIL-UC had over 4 million members. Garvey taught a love of Africa and of the African self. This was different than what a lot of Africans in the Diaspora were taught about their history and their culture at the time. Although Garvey and Du Bois were unrivalled innovators, Africans have always and everywhere resisted oppression, both in action and in theory. One might say that African-centredity stands on the shoulders of those who have come before. African-centredity builds on the work and struggles of radicals, activists, poets, scholars, and regular people in Africa and the Diaspora who have fought in their own ways against oppression: Frederick Douglas, Harriet Tubman, Booker T. Washington, Aimé Césaire, Amílcar Cabral, Rosa Parks, Viola Desmond, Martin Luther King, Jr., James Baldwin, Malcolm X, Nelson Mandela, and countless others.

In the 1960s and 1970s, scholars like Cheika Anta Diop, referring to the Continent (Africa), and Molefi Asante, examining the Diaspora (Africans living outside of the African continent), rose up to challenge the absence of African ideas, culture, and achievements in mainstream European, North American, and even African history. Building on the work of African-American and Caribbean thinkers before them, the new African-centred scholars argued that the accomplishments, history, and culture of Africans were central to human civilization. They also argued that African people everywhere needed the knowledge of their own important role in human history to overcome the racism and poverty facing many Africans around the world.

Doctor Frantz Fanon argued that history and culture are like parts of our body, like an arm or a leg, which for Africans have too often been amputated, separating people from important parts of who they are. Through a number of different processes such as slavery, voluntary immigration, and Eurocentric education, many African people have been cut off (or amputated) from the majestic history and culture of Africa and African people. One of the goals of African-centredity is to reconnect people to what has been taken away and denied by hundred of years of oppression. The better we understand the struggles and successes of our ancestors, the better prepared we are to understand the struggles of today and to work towards the successes of tomorrow.

Rather than seeking a superior position within a cultural hierarchy, African-centredity is a response to European cultural, political, economic, and social domination. African-centredity says no to Eurocentricity, especially as it relates to the lives, histories, and cultures of African peoples. Eurocentricity is part of a system that teaches the superiority of white European people, culture, history, and ideas over everything and everybody else. To this, African-centredity says "no, absolutely not". African-centredity asks us to take our eyes off Europe and its achievements. It also asks us to begin understanding the world with an eye for what is best for African (rather than European) peoples.

To better understand African-centredity, we must return to the definition from Molefi Asante. He begins by arguing that African-centredity is *"a mode of thought and action in which the centrality of African interests, values, and perspectives predominate."* This means that in order to take an African-centred approach, we have to consider what is best for African people. We also need to consider the notion of African values. Now, although this will vary from community to community, and from the Continent to the Diaspora, it is important to begin to think of what African values consist of.

There are a number of different approaches and sets of African values. What is critical is that we put African perspectives first, in both our actions and thought. To understand the idea of an African perspective, let us think of any historical event which has involved African people. For example, if we think of the European "discovery" of Africa, an African perspective might focus on the experience of Africans rather than the experience of Europeans. The rich white men, ones defined by European history as noble explorers and discovers, may have been viewed by Africans as violent thieves, invading the land populated by Africans as far back as anyone could remember. These two very different perspectives demonstrate that there are different ways to interpret historical events.

We can go back to Asante's definition. He continues: "In regards to theory, it is the placing of African people in the centre of any analysis of African phenomena. Thus, it is possible for anyone to master the discipline of seeking the location of Africans in a given phenomenon" (Asante 2003: 2). Asante is arguing that whenever we are writing, talking, or thinking about anything that has to do with Africa, we need to place African people in the centre of our scholarship. Asante is not saying that we should ignore everybody else, but where Africa is concerned, African people must be central and predominant in our minds and in the things we do. If we do this, he says, we will always be able to find and understand what a particular event or idea means to African peoples. We will also begin to understand what the impact of African people will be on the event or idea in question.

Asante's definition continues: "In terms of action and behaviour, it is a devotion to the idea that what is in the best interest of African consciousness is at the heart of ethical behaviour." In your schooling career, a number of people have probably told you what is right and what is wrong. Education in Canada is meant to teach ethical thought and action and is designed to provide you with a moral compass. African-centredity teaches that in order to be ethical in what we do and how we do it, we must work to improve our understanding of Africa and African perspectives. For Africans on the Continent and in the Diaspora, this is particularly important because by looking to Africa and African perspectives, African peoples everywhere are looking into their own histories, ideas, and identities. Because so much African history has been left out of "mainstream" schooling, Asante says it is a sort of ethical duty to re-centre that history and consciousness in our thoughts and actions.

"Finally, African-centredity seeks to enshrine the idea that blackness itself is a trope of ethics. Thus, to be Black is to be against all forms of oppression, racism, classism, homophobia patriarchy, child abuse, pedophilia, and white racial domination" (Asante 2003: 3). In this passage Asante is saying two major things. First, he is defining part of what it means to be Black. He says that to be Black is to not judge, punish or privilege people based on the colour of their skin, how much money they have, their sexual orientation, or their gender. To be Black, he says, is to never abuse or take advantage of a child, and to stop it whenever others may attempt such abuse. In fact, to be Black means standing against any unjust use of power by anyone anywhere. Of course, there are those within each ethno-racial group who contravene these ideals. Asante offers them as a moral calling. Asante's point is that to be Black is to be just, strong, and ethical. Asante, however, is doing more than just describing the meaning of being Black. Asante knows that most people often judge others for the wrong reasons. African-centredity calls Africans out to be better people: better to themselves and better to others through strength and righteousness. In summary, Asante is saying that to be Black is to bear a great responsibility; in fulfilling this responsibility, we fulfill the most important duties as leaders, followers, and members of our communities.

2.3 African-Canadians in History

As mentioned above, Africans are also one of the founding peoples of Canada and the United States. Before we discuss the founding of the nation, however, it is important to remember that the lands now called Canada and the United States were invaded, their people mostly killed, and their cultures, including the languages, spiritual practices, and ideas, banned. Although the Indigenous people of North America have always resisted European domination, like Africans in Africa, the technology and brutality of the European occupying invaders were often enough to overcome the people of this land. This early Canadian genocide, to cite one very troubling example, was not the doing of Canada's earliest Africans. The very first African Canadians did not arrive on our eastern shores voluntarily, nor did they choose to participate in the assault on Aboriginal peoples. The great majority of the earliest African Canadians were enslaved people, brought here by their European captors. This book uses the terms *enslaved person* and *enslaved people* instead of the terms slave or slaves. It is important to view the Africans who were stolen from their homes as what they were: hunters, carpenters, midwives, doctors, and farmers, to name just a selection of their roles. There has always been more to African lives and identities than slavery.

The first official record of an African person in Canada is that of Mathieu Da Costa in 1605. Although many who came after him would do so with shackles around their necks, feet, and hands, Da Costa was a free man (Speaks and Sweeney 1994). Some African Canadians can trace their history back sixteen generations. Despite a rich and long history in this country, Africans and African history still fall somehow outside the mainstream story of Canada. With so much missing from our history, it is easy to understand why some African Canadians feel like outsiders in Canadian society.

Many Canadians, as well as people of all ages, do not know that there was slavery in Canada. You may have been taught about the Underground Railroad and how many enslaved African Americans ran away from the United States to find freedom in Canada. What you may not know is that many of those who came found Canada less than welcoming. Many went back as soon as they could, and others organized boats back to Africa. Although Britain, and the territory now known as Canada, abolished slavery in 1833, many European Canadians were deeply racist. When the United States abolished slavery in 1865, many who had followed the Underground Railroad north, headed back. Canada was an unsafe and unwelcoming place for Africans fleeing the United States. The United States and Canada were both originally built on the sweat of enslaved Africans and the blood of Indigenous people.

With the abolishment of slavery in 1833, African Canadians were, like their brethren in the United States, not entirely free. Two sets of laws, rights, and realities existed between Black and white societies. Some people were freer than others. The history of African Canada is not simply the story of the domination of Blacks. It is a complex history of an intelligent, diverse, and resilient people who have struggled peacefully against violent oppression for a place in this nation. The following timeline demonstrates that, despite the obstacles before them, African Canadians resisted and persevered from the very beginning. As you read through the history of Africans in Canada as it is presented below, you should notice that this is a history of achievements, successes, and struggles. Although most schools in Canada and the United States do not teach Black history, those that do often choose February (Black History Month). Black History Month often focuses on slavery, oppression, and a few random inventions by African people in the United States and Canada. By the time you get through this timeline, you will see that even when the mainstream talks about African Canadians and African Canadian history, too much is omitted. If we call February Black History Month, what should we call the other months? Let us move away from designated months for Black, Aboriginal, Asian, women's, or LGBTTQ history to a curriculum informed by and infused with these histories.

*An African Canadian Timeline*http://www.dacosta400.ca/contact/contact.shtml

1600s–late 1700s	Enslaved African people were sold in Canada.
1605	Mattheu Da Costa, thought to be the first Black man in Canada (Acadia), came to Canada with Samuel de Champlain, the "Father of Canada". He travelled aboard the Jonas, which left La Rochelle, France, on May 13. Da Costa acted as an interpreter for the French among the Mi'kmaq natives. Clearly, he had been in Canada some time previous to Champlain's voyage of discovery, since Mi'kmaq is not a European or an African language.
1628	The first known enslaved African was recorded; a 6-year-old boy who was given the name of his owner, a priest named Olivier LeJeune.
1734	Marie Joseph Angelique, enslaved by de Franchville, a wealthy Montreal merchant, carried out a dramatic act of resistance. On April 17, after learning she was going to be sold, Marie Joseph set fire to her captor's house in order to cover her escape. The fire engulfed and destroyed forty-six buildings, including the Hotel Dieu. In June of 1734 she was captured, tortured, paraded through the streets, hanged, and her body burned as an example to others.
1780s	Shelburne, Nova Scotia was the site of Canada's first race riot. Members of the Black community were willing to work for less money than whites during a recession. Whites burned houses in the Black community in an attempt to discourage Blacks from working as cheap labourers.
1780s	Legislation was passed barring Black children from attending school. That legislation was only repealed during the early twentieth century.
1782–1785	About 3,500 Blacks fled to what is now Nova Scotia and New Brunswick at the close of the American Revolution. They had fought for Britain in return for freedom. Once in the Maritimes, they were cheated of land, forced to work on public projects such as road building, and denied equal status.
1783	A group called the Black Pioneers were some of the first settlers in Shelburne, Nova Scotia. They were men who had served in the army and had helped to build the town. They set up their own town called Birchtown, established by Colonel Stephen Blucke, near the outskirts of Shelburne. Although promised land by the British, they received only varying amounts of poor-quality land. Some received none at all.
1783	Rose Fortune became Canada's first Black policewoman in Annapolis Royal, Nova Scotia.
1784	There were 1,132 enslaved Blacks in Nova Scotia and New Brunswick, which made the total Black population 5,500 people.
1791	The British Government offered free passage to Blacks willing to relocate to the British colony of Sierra Leone.
1792	An exodus to Africa occurred: 1,190 men, women, and children left Halifax on 15 ships for the long voyage to Sierra Leone. Sixty-five died en route.
1792	A slave, attempting to enter a public hall, was struck dead with a spade. The killer stood trial but was later acquitted.
1793	Under the leadership of Lieutenant-Governor John Graves Simcoe, Upper Canada passed a law to stop people from bringing enslaved Africans into Upper Canada. The law also freed slaves who were 25 years of age or older. With this act, Upper Canada became the first British territory to bring in legislation against slavery, although it did not abolish it entirely.
1796	In July, nearly 600 Trelawney Maroons exiled from Jamaica arrived in Halifax, N.S. They faced miserable conditions in Canada. They opted to go to Sierra Leone in 1800.
1799	Louis-Joseph Papineau Sr. tried to re-establish slavery in Lower Canada.

2.3 African-Canadians in History

1800–1865	More than 30,000 Blacks found their way to Canada on the Underground Railroad. The Underground Railroad was a network of people who worked together to stage one of the largest – and most secret – uprisings in American history. Harriet Tubman, one of the most famous "conductors" on the Underground Railroad, spirited several hundred enslaved fugitives into Canada, despite a $40,000 reward for her capture, dead or alive.
1812	The first Baptist church was established in Colchester County, N.S.
1812	A Coloured Corps was formed during the War of 1812 after petitioning by Black veteran Richard Pierpoint.
1816	The Halifax Green Market Riots took place to protest racism.
1819	The Government of Upper Canada established the settlement of Oro for Black veterans of the War of 1812.
1820s–1840s	Black Canadians began playing an early form of ice hockey in Nova Scotia.
1833	The *British Imperial Act* abolished slavery in the British Empire (which included Canada), effective August 1, 1834.
1841	The British-American Institute was set up by Rev. Josiah Henson. It was a place where refugees could study and live. It is now in Dresden, Ontario.
1844	The African Baptist Church in Dartmouth, N.S. was founded on June 9.
1846	In Ontario, the *Common Schools Act* was passed, allowing separate schools for Blacks and Roman Catholics. This resulted in many whites refusing to have their children attend schools with Blacks.
1848	William Brown Sr. purchased the first property in Africville, N. S., a traditionally Black community.
1850	The second *Fugitive Slave Act* was passed in the United States, placing all people of African descent at risk. The Underground Railroad increased its operations.
1850	With aid from the Presbyterian Church, the Eglin settlement, a Black settlement, was created in Ontario.
1852	Nova Scotia's William Hall, age 12, enlisted in the Royal Navy and served on the flagship Victory, becoming the first African-Canadian sailor.
1853	Mary Ann Shadd, the first Black journalist and newspaper publisher in Canada, launched *The Provincial Freeman*, one of two Black newspapers published in Ontario from 1853 to 1857. Shadd was the first Black newspaperwoman and the first woman publisher of a newspaper in Canada.
1854–1860	Septimus Clarke served as the first clerk of the African Baptist Association.
1857	William Hall became the first person of African descent to receive the Victoria Cross for bravery and distinguished service.
1858	The discovery of gold, well-publicized along the west coast, attracted hundreds of fortune seekers to Victoria and to the banks of the Fraser River. The steamship *Commodore* brought the first wave of Black gold-hunters from San Francisco to Esquimalt, B.C. on April 25.
1860	The Black military group, the Victoria Rifle Corps, were ready to defend British Columbia if needed.
1861	Dr. Anderson Ruffin Abbott became Canada's first doctor of African descent.
1869	Black businessman Mifflin Gibbs was a member of Victoria's municipal government.
1870	Lester and Gibbs, a general store, was set up in Victoria, B.C. by two Black businessmen, Mifflin Gibbs and Peter Lester.
1870	John Hamilton invented the first railway flanger, used to keep rails free of snow and slush.
1872	Elijah McCoy, born in Colchester, Ontario, invented the first of his many devices for oil engines used in trains and factories. His inventions were so good that many people refused to have imitations of his work. They insisted (and still insist) on having "the real McCoy".

1880	Mary Ann Shadd organized the Coloured Women's Progressive Association.
1882	A Black cowboy, John Ware, introduced longhorn cattle into Canada. He also was one of the first people to start rodeo riding.
1885	Delos Roget Davis, of Amherstberg, Ontario, became one of Ontario's first Black lawyers. He was appointed to the King's Council in 1910.
1890	Known as "the greatest little fighter the world has ever known", George Dixon won the world's featherweight championship in 1890.
1893	Henry Sylvester Williams enrolled at Dalhousie University in Halifax.
1894	William Peyton Hubbard became the first Black council member elected to Toronto City Council, and was re-elected for 13 successive terms. He served on the Board of Control and acted as mayor on a number of occasions.
1895	The *Acadian Recorder* reported on the first official Black hockey league.
1900	The Coloured Women's Club of Montréal was founded.
1904	The Coloured Hockey League played its last year as a major entity.
1905	The "Black Trek", the migration of dissatisfied African-Americans from Oklahoma to the Canadian prairies, began.
1905	A group led by W.E.B. DuBois and Monroe Trotter met secretly in Niagara, Ontario to organize to resist racism in the United States.
1907	Canada restricted immigration.
1907	The predominantly African-Canadian Union United Church was formed in Montréal.
1909	Many people in the West were outraged at the number of Black people moving into the Canadian West and had the immigration laws changed, making it more difficult for Black people to immigrate to the West.
1910	The first Black person to be appointed to the King's Council in Ontario was Delos Rogest Davis of Amherstburg.
1916	The No. 2 Construction Battalion was formed in Nova Scotia.
1919	Most railway porters were Black men who formed the Brotherhood of Sleeping Car Porters.
1920s	Hundreds of Caribbean immigrants, called the "later arrivals", flocked to Cape Breton, N.S., to work in coal mines and a steel factory.
1922	The last recorded game of the Africville Sea-Sides was played against the Halifax All-Stars.
1925	Oscar Peterson, Canada's most famous jazz musician, was born.
1929	Rockhead's Paradise, an important entertainment centre, was opened in Montréal by Black entrepreneur Rufus Rockhead.
1930s	There was massive unemployment among Blacks during the Depression.
1933	Gordon T.C. Jemmott, former star and coach of the Africville Brown Bombers, became the new headmaster at the Africville School.
1939–1945	Many Blacks enlisted in the armed forces to fight for Canada during World War II, in spite of opposition from authorities. Blacks insisted on serving their country, however, and eventually joined all services.
1946–1956	Nova Scotia's first Black newspaper, *The Clarion*, was founded and published in New Glasgow by Carrie Best. Carrie Best used *The Clarion* to publicize the case of Viola Desmond, a Black Halifax businesswoman who was arrested for violating the "no-Blacks" rule by sitting in the whites-only seats in the Roseland Theatre in New Glasgow, N.S. The publicity brought to Mrs. Desmond's case, thanks in a large part to the attention of Best, helped abolish the laws permitting Black segregation in Nova Scotia.
1947	Jackie Robinson broke baseball's colour barrier in Montréal.
1948	The first Black women to graduate from a Canadian School of Nursing were Gwyneth Barton and Ruth Bailey.
1950s	New laws made it illegal to refuse people work, withhold service in stores or restaurants, or prevent someone from moving into a home because of race.

2.3 African-Canadians in History

1950s	The Victoria General Nursing Hospital did not accept Black students until the mid-1950s.
1951	Porters on the Northern Alberta Railway were unionized.
1952	The first Black woman to be ordained to the ministry was Reverend Addie Aylestock.
1953	The Africville School was closed.
1953	Wilson Brooks, an RCAF Veteran, became Toronto's first Black public school teacher.
1956	The report recommending the annexation of Africville land was published by the City of Halifax.
1958	Willie O'Ree became the first Black hockey player in the National Hockey League.
1959	Stanley Grizzle was the first Black person to run for a seat in the Ontario Legislature.
1960s	Community-wide segregation of Blacks existed throughout Nova Scotia until the 1960s. Restaurants, churches, and movie theatres were segregated.
1960s	Senator Calvin Rucke established a housing co-op in East Preston, N.S. that enabled Black people to own their homes.
1962	The Ontario Human Rights Commission, the first in Canada, was formed. Its first director was American-born Black activist Daniel G. Hill, who moved to Canada in 1950. It was the first government agency in Canada established to protect citizens from discrimination. Hill later became chair of the Commission.
1963	Lionel Jones was the first Black man to be admitted to the Bar in Alberta.
1963	An African-Canadian man, Calvin Best of Nova Scotia, became the president of the Civil Service Association of Canada.
1963	Leonard Braithwaite was elected to the Ontario legislature. He was the first African-Canadian to serve in a provincial legislature in Canada.
1964	A Québec law was passed forbidding discrimination in employment.
1964	Leonard Braithwaite participated in the amendment of the *Separate Schools Acts*, leading to the end of segregation in schools.
1965	The last segregated school, in Essex County, Ontario, closed.
1967	The last of the residents of Africville were relocated.
1968	Portia White, a famed classical singer, died at the age of 57.
1969	The Sir George Williams University's Computer Department in Montreal was occupied in a protest against inequality. This school was the forerunner of Concordia University.
1969	The first Black police officer in Regina was David Pollanis.
1969	The first Black man to become a member of the federal parliament was Lincoln Alexander of Ontario.
1969	The first national Black organization was formed in Ontario. It was called the National Black Coalition of Canada.
1969	The first Black lawyer to be admitted to the Bar in British Columbia was Ed Searles.
1969	The first Black History Week was celebrated.
1969	The City of Halifax began to bulldoze Africville.
1970	Aaron "Pa" Carvery was the last man standing at Africville on January 2.
1972	The first Black members of the British Columbia legislature were Rosemary Brown and Emery Barnes.
1974	The first Black man to be elected mayor was Dr. Monestine Saint Firmin of Mattawa, Ontario.
1974	The first Black moderator of the United Church of Canada was Dr. Wilbur Howard of Ontario.
1975	Canada's first Black federal citizenship court judge was Stanley G. Grizzle.
1978	The Ontario Black History Society was founded by Dr. Daniel Hill, Wilson Brooks, and Lorraine Hubbard. The Society was dedicated to the acknowledgement and preservation of Black contributions to Canada's development.
1980	Lincoln Alexander retired from Parliament and became the chairman of the Ontario Workmen's Compensation Board.

1983	Elnora Collins, a noted singer, received an Achievement Award from the Black Historical and Cultural Society in British Columbia for her contribution to the entertainment industry.
1983	The Black Cultural Centre for Nova Scotia opened.
1985	Makeda Silvera became the co-founder and managing editor of Sister Vision Press, the first press for Black women in Canada.
1985	Daurene Lewis, the first Black female mayor of this town, took the oath on January 3 in Annapolis Royal, Nova Scotia.
1986	Anne John-Baptiste, member of the Focus on Black Women group, served as a parliamentary assistant for New Democrat MP Dan Heap.
1986	The National Organization of Immigrant and Visible Minority Women of Canada was formed in Winnipeg. The organization was created to deal with language barriers, racism, immigration, mental health, and work conditions.
1991	Julius Alexander Isaac, a native of Grenada, was named Chief Justice of the Federal Court of Canada. He was the first Black Chief Justice in Canada and the first to serve on the Federal Court.
1993	Jean Augustine was sworn in as Canada's first Black female Member of Parliament.
1997	Dionne Brand was given the Governor-General's Award for Poetry and the Trillium Award for Literature for her work *Land To Light On*.
2001	Alison Duke was given the award for Best Canadian Documentary at the Reel World Film Festival for her rap documentary *Raisin' Kane*.
2005	Michelle Jean was sworn in as Canada's first Black female Governor General.
2009	Barack Obama is elected President of the United States.
2009	Toronto District School Board introduces an African-centred elementary school.

The following lesson plan offers suggestions for using the African Canadian Timeline to engage students.

Lesson Title: Tracing Our Timelines

Curriculum Expectations: Teachers will refer to the relevant curriculum expectations. This lesson may apply to History, Social Studies, Media, and English courses.

Description/Lesson Objective: Students will continue to build upon their African-centred knowledge and critical thinking skills by examining the parallels between personal and societal events.

Materials Required: Students will be provided with a copy of the African Canadian Timeline.

Planning Notes: Teachers are invited to liaise with Teacher-Librarians, local historians, history societies, and community activists to provide access to relevant resources.

Accommodations:

- Review with colleagues from the Special Education and Guidance Departments to determine effective and relevant strategies to support student learning.
- Pre-teach vocabulary.
- Provide copies of teacher's notes, as requested, by students.
- Provide accessible copies of handouts.
- Arrange for students to have study peers.
- Provide additional time for students to write material from the board.

2.3 African-Canadians in History

Equitable Teaching/Learning Activities:

- Ask students to complete a personal timeline featuring key moments in their lives. Events to include:
  - your birthdate;
  - when you took your first steps;
  - when you graduated from elementary school;
  - when you got your driver's license;
  - when you plan to graduate from high school.

Sample Timeline:
Start
(Birth)

- Have students compare their timelines with each other.
- The teacher writes his/her timeline on the board. Invite students to see similarities and differences between their timelines and the teacher's timeline.
- The teacher explains how History uses timelines to identify key moments and people.
- The teacher writes a selection of events from the timeline on the board and provides a brief explanation of each event. The students consider how one event might lead to another.
- The students select what they feel are the three most important historic contributions from the timeline and complete the following visual organizer.

Event selected	Summary	What is historically important
Event #1:		
Event #2:		
Event #3:		

- The students research each of these events in the school library and the community. If possible, the teacher may wish to invite local community activists and historians to share their insights about the timeline and to consider why these facts might have been omitted from the official curriculum.
- Writing in role, the students present a historic account of the life, times, and significance of the historic event they feel is most important from the timeline. They may present their findings in one of the following forms:
  - Diary entries
  - Letters
  - Dramatic monologue
  - Song
  - Panel discussion with other students
  - Research essay

- ○ Portfolio with text and visuals
- ○ Website
- ○ Poster, drawing, or other visual depiction

Assessment and Evaluation Strategies:

- The teacher circulates around the classroom to listen to and provide assistance to students while they research the top three choices.
- The teacher may wish to collect the completed visual organizers and provide feedback to students.
- Students complete a rough draft of their work and receive assessment (feedback) from the teacher prior to submitting the final version for evaluation.

Teacher Reflections: To be completed at the end of the lesson.

2.4 Conclusion

It is important to remember that African-centredity is firmly rooted in Africa – in its traditions, histories, practices, and people. Although Molefi Asante provides the most well-known version of the theory, even he lets us know that it is African scholars like Cheika Anta Diop who, among others, provide the foundations upon which African-centredity stands. As you read through the text, you will hopefully come back to this chapter and wonder how anyone could have ignored such a marvellous history. Perhaps feeling as Asante did, you know that new ways of understanding, living, and seeing are necessary to connect with a past from which we have become so tragically removed. By understanding the connection between today's African communities in the Diaspora and Africans on the continent, we redefine our understanding of the world and our place in it. By understanding the relationship between our contemporary lives and the proud history of Africa and it peoples, we redefine the meaning of Africa in our minds, our conceptions of what it means to be Black, our links to Diaspora, and how non-Blacks may become allies for this history and tradition.

African-centredity relies upon roots planted deep in the African soil, roots that take us all the way back to the beginning of human kind. African-centredity stems from the culture, history, and geography of Africa – a culture and history that are today global. We cannot speak of African civilization in the twenty-first Century without mentioning the countless groups and individuals in the global African Diaspora. This textbook intends not only to teach you about the history and present of Africa and African peoples but also to connect you to these histories. Most students have been disconnected from most world history, including Latin American, Asian, and Africans, as if someone has unplugged the TV and the picture has disappeared. For most of us, the only TV still plugged in runs a 24-h a day show about European culture and history. This book hopes to reconnect the power and show you not just a different programme but also a new way of seeing. We have not only been watching the Europe show, but we have been watching it in a European way. African-centredity hopes to give you new eyes – no matter who you are – for seeing and understanding the world around us. The focus of this discussion has been on placing Africa, African peoples, and their interests at the centre of the living history we describe in this book. Finally, African-centredity is not a perfect theory. It will not solve all the problems of the world or even all of those facing Africans on the Continent and in the Diaspora. Like any well-known idea, it has its critics and it has its limitations. This textbook is a tool for guiding our approach to writing and understanding African history. We offer African-centredity to you as a companion for reading and working with this book. What you do with the ideas of African-centredity outside of your use of this book is completely up to you. Chapter 3 offers a selection of ideas. By expanding this knowledge, Chapter 3 links approaches to the study of Africa to practical applications for teachers and students.

References

Asante, MK. (2003). *Afrocentricity: The Theory of Social Change.* Chicago: African American Images.

Ontario Ministry of Education and Training. (1993). *Antiracism and Ethnocultural Equity in School Boards: Guidelines for Policy Development and Implementation.* Toronto: Queen's Printer for Ontario.

Ontario Ministry of Education and Training. (1999). *The Ontario Curriculum, Grades 9 and 10: English.* Toronto: Queen's Printer for Ontario.

Ontario Ministry of Education and Training. (2000a). *The Ontario Curriculum, Grades 11 and 12: Classical Studies and International Languages.* Toronto: Queen's Printer for Ontario.

Ontario Ministry of Education and Training. (2000b). *The Ontario Curriculum, Grades 11 and 12: Social Sciences and Humanities.* Toronto: Queen's Printer for Ontario.

Ontario Ministry of Education and Training. (2003). *The Ontario Secondary School Literacy Course (OSSLC), Grade 12.* Toronto: Queen's Press for Ontario.

Ontario Ministry of Education and Training. (2005a). *The Ontario Curriculum, Grades 9 and 10, Canadian and World Studies.* Toronto: Queen's Printer for Ontario.

Ontario Ministry of Education and Training. (2005b). *The Ontario Curriculum Grades 11 and 12 Revised: Canadian and World Studies.* Toronto: Queen's Printer for Ontario.

Ontario Ministry of Education and Training. (2009). *Equity and Inclusive Education Strategy.* Toronto: Queen's Printer for Ontario.

Public District School Board Writing Partnership. (2002). *Course Profile, Philosophy: Questions and Theories, Grade 12, University Preparation, HZT4U.* Toronto: Queen's Printer for Ontario.

Speaks, A. & Sweeney, S. (1994). *Hymn to Freedom.* (Video recording). Hamilton: Almeta Speaks Productions, Inc.

Chapter 3
The Study of Africa and the African Experience: The Challenge and Possibilities of an Integrative Theory

Abstract Resisting hierarchies of identification and knowledge, this discussion grounds the argument for African-centred schooling within the epistemological approach of integrative theory. In seeing teaching, learning, and identity formation as interconnected political processes, an African-centred approach provides a space for the consideration of a holistic approach to equitable instruction and subjectivity.

Keywords Africa · Integrative theory · Teaching · Learning · Interconnections · Holistic education · Equity · Diversity · Identity formation · Students

3.1 Introduction

In this chapter, I attempt to broaden the Afroscopic lens to the study of Africa by integrating an anti-colonial discursive framework with an African-centred approach to teaching and learning about the African experience. The learning objective is twofold. First, I intend to show the power of an eclectic theoretical approach to understanding contemporary Africa. This approach moves us beyond simply "studying Africa" to a critical appreciation of current struggles, challenges, constraints, and possibilities of an imagined future in a global community. Second, an integrative theoretical approach allows us to engage some of the contemporary issues that connect Africa, Diasporan experiences, and the global challenges of "development". This approach seeks to consider how to teach the African experience in ways beneficial to the cause of African and minority education in North American contexts.

Recalling our first forays into African history and historiography at the start of this text, the reader was asked to ponder the relevance of theoretical prisms to understanding Africa. Teaching and learning about Africa is about understanding the totality of a people's lived experiences. There are intellectual lenses to use in coming to a critical understanding of the complexities of the challenges, struggles, successes, and failures of a people. Critical teaching and learning about Africa and the African experience require the development of new and inclusive theoretical prisms (ways of seeing). In this chapter, I argue for an anti-colonial theoretical approach to strengthen the African-centred lens for the study of Africa and African issues.

Theoretically, this book adopts a critical anti-colonial discursive framework to understand the issues of culture, social difference, identity, and representation in schooling and the implications for genuine educational options in an African context. "Colonial" is conceptualized not simply as "foreign" or "alien" but rather as "imposed and dominating". As noted already, the anti-colonial framework is a theorization of issues emerging from colonial relations (Fanon 1963; Memmi 1969; Foucault 1980). The anti-colonial approach recognizes the importance of locally produced knowledge emanating from cultural history, daily human experiences, and social interactions.

In proposing a critical anti-colonial stance to teaching and learning about Africa I am relying on three writers: Fanon (1967) on the violence of colonization, Memmi (1969) on the relations between the colonized and the colonizer, and Cabral (1970) on the personal toll of colonialism and the need for resistance. Anti-colonial theorizing also stresses the local knowings of the colonized, the recourse to power, and subjective agency for resistance. Knowledge emerges from where people are situated. This means understanding knowledge from multiple sites and sources: formal, informal, and non-formal learning cultures. Knowledge is socially, culturally, and politically relevant if it maintains a fit with people's aspirations, lived experiences, and practices. The anti-colonial discursive framework allows for research to highlight issues and questions about knowledge production, identity, and representation in schooling and education in diverse contexts. It draws out insights of local knowledge, individual agency, power, and resistance for rethinking schooling and education in African and North American contexts. Everyday events and lived experiences of peoples are to be analysed in the context of the identities of the local subjects and the particular historical experiences they bring to their own environments.

Anti-colonial theory also moves beyond critique to new visions of society (see Dei and Kempf 2006; Kempf 2009). Education has a key role to play in this task. Education must provide learners with the tools to understand and transform society. The demands and requirements of contemporary schooling and education in the global era must achieve the following: cultivate and promote the cultures, national identities, and heritage of learners; ensure that the learner can function well in a global competitive market; and be able to demonstrate competence in local cultural knowledge and language. Anti-colonial theory explores the possibilities of bringing about meaningful changes that respond to these challenges.

Certain forms of knowledge have traditionally been devalued and denied access into the educational system. Yet such knowledge holds lessons for change, and educators must search for ways to introduce these ways of seeing as part of the multiplicity of knowing. Local and Indigenous educators must begin to appreciate their own Indigeneity and local knowledge in order to teach and bring such knowledge into schools. We may begin to see how anti-colonial educational practice may focus

3.1 Introduction

on power relations of knowledge production and create spaces for counterinsurgent voices to be heard.

Difference is central to anti-colonial theorizing about community. Understanding Africa as a site of difference has implications for how schools engage knowledge – via teaching and learning – about African peoples and their experiences. The issues of difference and the effects on schooling play out differently in varying contexts. In North American schooling, for example, difference is affirmed, though educators have not necessarily responded to difference. The acknowledgement of difference has not always led to educators and schools instituting measures that concretely address the implications of difference. Responding to difference would also require that educators address the power-saturated issues of schooling, since difference itself provides the context for power and domination. Similarly, African education has fundamentally been approached as a matter of national development. In emphasizing the goal of national integration, "post-colonial" education in Africa has denied difference in local populations, as if difference itself was a problem.

The current school system, particularly in Europe, North America, and the Diaspora in general, basically operates within "the cult of individualism". Individual achievement, excellence, and merit are celebrated. This approach goes against the tenets of a "community of learners" and "collective responsibility". Those who do well in the system, notably the high academic achievers, often see no obligation to those who are "struggling". The prevailing understanding is that those who do well do so as a result of their individual hard work and personal effort and not through the collective learning process. Consequently, "academic failure" is an individual problem. A different interpretation, one working with philosophical understandings of "community of learners", would see failure as a collective problem. Achieving success is also a collective undertaking. For success to be meaningful it must be holistic. It must acknowledge the collective contributions of the community of learners. Success and failure must also be consequential for the community of learners in the educational system. The merit and reward badges of schooling militate against this critical understanding of educational achievement. Thus, to have "success" there must be "failures".

It is this absence of understanding the community and collective responsibility in schooling and education that an anti-colonial prism to understanding education hopes to address. Power is evoked to address the broad concerns of a community of learners. Schools train citizens to care for society and communities. Education is for both personal growth and collective improvement. Education should be about breaking down barriers and boundaries, about equity in excellence. In looking at the production of failure in the current school systems, one must evoke different readings of "social justice" and "inclusion" in education. There is no justice in education when some students are either failing by conventional standards of measurements or are being failed by the system. Working with alternative views of social justice would recognize this shared responsibility. By appropriating the progressive discourse of equity through the now popular refrain of "standards", "measurements", "accountability", "quality", "responsibility", "individualism", "systemic neglect", and "institutional culpability" are being silenced.

Similarly, our understanding of "inclusion" must shift. Inclusion cannot be discussed in the absence of a politics of accountability and transparency located in a community ethic. The community is made up of individuals and the ties that bind them. Community does not mean the absence of heterogeneity or difference. More importantly, "inclusion" cannot be defined in the prism of adding to what already exists. An alternative conception calls for beginning anew. Why? This is because what already exists is the source of the problem in the first place. With this understanding is a basic philosophic tenet of an anti-colonial prism to understanding African education.

So what do we mean then by "inclusivity"? There are different interpretations of inclusivity. In North American and diasporic contexts there are two strands: first, there is a focus on special education and, particularly, students with learning disabilities; second, there is a broader view of inclusion that highlights questions of power and social difference. In the African context, inclusive schooling is a relatively recent concept with a focus on special education. This stems from a failure to acknowledge difference as a significant site for schooling and education, as well as an erroneous conceptualization that students who have been traditionally excluded have been those with profound learning disabilities and in need of special assistance. The position is that we need inclusive education to accommodate these students.

A more critical and holistic understanding of inclusion is about ensuring that schools are welcoming for all and particularly respond to the needs and concerns of a diverse body politic. This means addressing questions of difference, diversity, and power as defined through the lenses of class, ethnicity, gender, disability, sexuality, religion, and language. Hence, the idea of students with "learning difficulties or disabilities" is understood as a systemic, structural, and instructional problem of conventional schooling. Such analysis shifts the focus away from the individual learner to the structures of educational delivery. Inclusion is about working with difference as sites of strength and power inequities. We need a better understanding that extends the discussion beyond the bland talk of inclusion – the add and stir approach – to dealing with power, accountability, and transparency issues of schooling. Inclusion is also about defining "schooling" broadly, as something beyond the four-walled classroom, to encompass teachers and students. It is about dealing with the erasures, negations, and omissions in conventional schooling.

As pointed out elsewhere (Dei 2007) an anti-colonial approach to teaching Africa must engage such issues as the multiple ways of producing, interrogating, and validating knowledge. Difference is clearly relevant to understanding everyday practices of schooling; yet, it is one aspect of the discourse on schooling that has been neglected in teachings of African schooling and education. African schooling is a process and a practice mediated by the powerful intersections of ethnicity, class, gender, language, religion, sexuality, and culture. An inclusive schooling system is one that is capable of responding to ethnic, cultural, linguistic, sexually orientated, and religious differences among the community of learners. Inclusive schooling is about a demonstrated commitment to address the diverse needs of all students. It requires an acknowledgement of the historical and institutional structures and contexts that sustain educational inequities in schools.

Through colonial and colonizing relations of schooling social inequities can be perpetuated. An anti-colonial prism to teaching about Africa is understanding difference as both a site of knowledge and a source of exclusionary practice in schools. Although concepts such as race, ethnicity, gender, culture, sexuality, religion, and language are social constructions, they have real material and political effects on the schooling processes for all learners. These identities are constructed differently over time, as are their real effects. Ethnic differences are significant in that they carry powerful political and material effects for people who can be advantaged or disadvantaged on the basis of their ethnic affiliations. Similarly, learners' bodies are marked by gender, sexuality, class, linguistic, and religious differences, each of which carries currency in the social setting. To overly simplify one's identity denies a part of the self. The non-recognition of an aspect of one's identity is equally oppressive (Taylor 1994:25).

In fact, the denial of ethnicity in African schooling is also seen in the avoidance of race in North America. Ethnicity is a troubling issue given the politics of colonization and the history of colonial education (Bassey 1999; Brock-Utne 1996, 2000). Ethnicity evokes a colonial history of distinctions, which fosters unhealthy tensions and competition among groups and communities with interrelated histories. This "divide and rule" tactic formed part of the pre-colonial administration. Unfortunately, the post-colonial era has not succeeded in addressing this issue. In some cases, the problem has been intensified. Teaching critically about Africa must engage the asymmetrical power relations that structure the lives of learners. The tensions between educating for nation building and recognizing difference are not endemic to African communities. These tensions are located in the relations of schooling. The creation of a shared national identity has been viewed in conflict with support for various ethnicities and their cultures. The schooling community is a community of differences. These differences need to be affirmed (rather than denied) to strengthen community building. For educators to work with ethnicity and difference in positive (i.e. solution-oriented) ways, we must uphold the virtues of difference and deal with the asymmetrical power relations in the classroom. Critical education can foster a shared sense of identity and collective belonging. Critically teaching about Africa must interrogate the anti-colonial politics of nation building. Today we must be wary of the "fear of difference" (Dei 2007).

3.2 The African-Centred Educational Philosophy as Anticolonial

Borrowing from the pioneering work of Asante (1980), Asante (1991a,b), Asante (1992), the African-centred principles include notions of community, responsibility, mutual interdependence, spirituality in education, the link of identity (race/ethnicity, class, gender, sexuality, [dis]ability, language, religion, and culture) in education, history, and heritage. By community and responsibility we mean the sense of belonging in unison with others and an expectation of obligations to the survival and sanctity of the individual and community. It means maintaining one's individuality while recognizing the primacy of the communal ties and the responsibilities that come with such membership. Schooling is a community of learners; therefore, it requires mutual obligations and responsibilities among learners. Individual rights are affirmed to the extent that they further the project of community or collective survival. Such rights are only meaningful with accompanying responsibilities. The idea of mutual interdependence recognizes that the success of one depends on others. No one can go or do it alone (see also Hilliard 1992; Karenga 1986, 1988).

Spirituality in education connects the self to the community in terms of a tie beyond the capacity of the human senses. It is about a wholeness of education embracing the fusion of body, mind, and soul. Spiritual identities provide the emotional and psychological strength to the learner. They can be called upon to resolve tensions and the material damages inflected by schooling and education. Spirituality in education then becomes survival and resistance. We connect identity (race, class, gender, sexuality, disability, language, religion, etc.) to schooling and knowledge production because learners come to school and engage the learning process with their bodies. There is an embodiment of knowledge which is also a form of knowledge consciousness arising from the experience, histories, and subjectivity that shape everyday action. Identity is also taken as complex, political, and refracted in asymmetrical power relations in schooling. The different and multiple bodies and social relations of schooling are seen as structured in asymmetrical power relations.

Given that identity is political, a teaching identity is about resistance. While history is about the totality of lived experience, African-centred educational philosophy, history, and heritage are evoked as parts of knowledge that inform the experiences of a people, its past, its present, and its future. Histories, while different, are seen as intertwined or connected. The particularity of a history is connected with the collective experiences shared by a people. African-centred educational philosophy reclaims the past as a necessary exercise in decolonization for the learner. It also reflects on the present in terms of understanding contemporary challenges and complexities. African-centred education helps project into and contest the future by way of thinking through possible solutions to the challenges dictated by a people's own history, culture, and experiences. Critical education is intended to affirm the learner's culture, history, and local/Indigenous languages. African-centred teachings privilege the principles of communalism, solidarity, and responsibility. The educational goal is the development of the whole child, emphasizing cognitive, affective, and psychomotor domains of the learner.

The difference between an African-centred educational philosophy and the inclusive schooling context is that the latter fails to ground these philosophical values and ideals in the education of the youth. Often issues are treated superficially as inclusion is added to what already exists without challenging Eurocentric education. Issues of racism, ethnocentrism, sexism, classism, ableism, and homophobia may be discussed at the individual and episodic levels; however, these may be left to the whims and caprices of an educator without acknowledging the systemic, structural, and institutional contexts of social oppression and how schools themselves help reproduce social inequities. Culture can be depoliticized and issues of identity can

3.2 The African-Centred Educational Philosophy as Anticolonial

be taken up without discussions of power, privilege, and institutional complicities in maintaining social dominance.

African-centred educational philosophy enhances inclusive education. It complements inclusive schooling if the issues specified as providing the philosophical grounding for African-centred education are taken up in a way that centres multiple learners from where they are coming from. Given the diversity of learners, they will be differently grounded in terms of where they are coming from. No one centre becomes dominant. The politics of African-centred education creates the room for multi-centric forms of education to flourish. In fact, the survival of the African-centred knowledge depends on cultivating this sense of multi-centric knowledges as it alone (African-centredity) cannot challenge the dominance of Eurocentric knowledge. This recognition is a paradigmatic shift away from the universalistic claim "to know" that is made by dominant knowledge forms. By centring the learner in her/his own experience, history, perspective, understanding, and interpretation, a different knowing emerges similar to the noted fusion of body, mind, and soul in defining the learner's identity. This "centring" helps learners become creative agents with active/resistant voices telling their own stories (see Dei 1996a,b).

The fact that African-centred knowledge does not masquerade as universal knowing is a major distinguishing aspect from Eurocentric knowledge. African-centred educational philosophy recognizes the power of other ways of knowing emerging from the space of cultural specificities. It does not negate, devalue, or dismiss other ways of knowing. The critique of Eurocentric knowledge by African-centred proponents is about the former's devaluation of other knowledges rather than a dismissing of the place of Eurocentric knowing in multiple knowledge forms. Contrary to its critics, African-centred educational philosophy is not premised on the unconditional affirmation of African culture. It recognizes the validity and relevance of African culture as a legitimate source of knowledge.

African-centred educational philosophy reveals an African world view and points to the relevance of such a world view in a diasporic context. A world view is about a cosmos or cosmo-vision, a way of looking at the world. This view is about how a community makes meaning of the interface between the physical and metaphysical realms. An African-centred world view is not monolithic but embraces certain shared ideas and values. An African-centred world view embraces the rich philosophical traditions of African peoples encapsulated in culture, history, and heritage. Such a world view sees the human world as fundamentally spiritual. Yet the material world does not stand apart from the metaphysical and spiritual worlds. There is an interrelationship between the material, physical, and metaphysical realms. The knowledge base ascribes to a peaceful co-existence between culture and nature. Not uniquely African, and shared by most Indigenous peoples, this world view forms a fundamental aspect of human existence and social relationships. An African world view privileges understandings of community over individual, responsibility over rights, mutual interdependence over competitive spirit, spirituality over the mundane or secular in the everyday existence, and a belief in the power of ancestors as guardians over the living. In an African-centred world view, practice and experience are seen as the contextual bases of knowledge. Knowledge is accumulative and based on an empirical observation of the universe. It can be transmitted intergenerationally as well as through vision and dreams. Knowledge can be embodied. In the diasporic context, peoples of African descent can work with these rich philosophical values and historical traditions. This means developing a knowledge base informed by a sense of community belonging, social responsibility, traditions of mutuality, creating a space for the spiritual in the material world, and developing respect and veneration for ancestors and ancestral knowledge.

Despite the variety of cultures, diasporic social thought is based on the core values of community, social responsibility, traditions of mutuality, spiritual base of human existence, and interrelations. Diasporic social thought is essentially a political, cultural-ideological frame of reference linked to notions of culture, identity, freedom, and liberation to ensure and sustain the development of African peoples. The goal of this framework is to bring peoples of African descent together to forge a common front politically, economically, spiritually, and socially. It seeks to teach the history and culture of the people of Africa and African descent, allowing Africans in the Diaspora to identify with the continent, forging bonds of community and identity, and placing Africa on an equal footing with other cultures. Diasporic social thought also celebrates Africa's humanism and rich heritage as counterpoints to European racism and colonialism (Konadu 2006). In fact, one of the greatest contributions of Africa to world knowledge is the "African humanism" – the African love and generosity for humanity, the interrelations of rights and responsibilities, and the connections of the individual to community (Du Bois 1947, 1969). African humanism espouses the ethical ideals of social justice and a concern for collective human good in the world. This humanism is also an ethical and spiritual tradition, as Karenga (2007: 7) notes, demanding that African peoples "care for the vulnerable, support social change and continue the historical struggles for freedom and rights of all humans". Diasporic social thought seeks a rebirth, a revival of African culture, a return to historical traditions, and a new paradigm for the future by looking at the past to chart the future for Africa. The interrogation and scrutiny of African cultures and cultural values, history, and tradition are necessary for cultivating in youth a change in attitudes, self-dependence, and self-pride. This framework also calls for return to the African roots for self-definition and taking African cultural perspectives seriously to explore new ways of doing things and what is working.

African-centred schooling and education have the goal of helping African learners and youth reinvent their Africanness in a diasporic context. The pursuit of African education must be about understanding what our identities mean to us and the politics required in making such identifications. African-centred schooling and education must help African youth assert themselves in the political, psychological, cultural, artistic, and creative spheres. Such education seeks to enable today's youth to deploy Africanness/Blackness as a positive concept, be proud of their ancestry, discover the beauty of Blackness/Africanness, and become conscious of their own historical situation. This is relevant as there continues to be a threat to the destruction of African identities. Society and its institutions are daily asking African youth to amputate a part of themselves and/or to renounce the pride of one's color. This is why we need a spiritually grounded approach to education to deal with youth alienation from current schooling environments. African-centred schooling and education address the misrepresentation of our identities and communities in the Diaspora.

A school's curriculum may espouse an African-centred educational philosophy to the extent that it speaks of the experiences, histories, and cultures of African peoples in their complexities and diversities. The school curriculum is more than the texts/textual materials. It is about the wholeness of education. An African-centred curriculum is holistic. It is about textual, instructional, and pedagogic practices, as well as officially specified rules, regulations, and procedures that provide a character for the school and connects the school with the broader community. As noted in Dei et al. (1995; 1997), the African-centred school operates with a "deep curriculum" by noting and working with the intersection of the culture/climate, social environments, and organizational life of the school. Given that what counts as "curriculum" is socially determined/constructed, the African-centred curriculum must be seen as a powerful knowledge system of African peoples themselves. Anything else is not African-centred. Giroux (1981) long ago pointed out that the curriculum is a particular ordering of social knowledge. Educators must see curriculum as a path to follow or course of action in schooling. African-centred curriculum in this regard is political. It charts a course for promoting African youth education as a primary objective.

We must be able to evaluate the appropriateness of African-centred curriculum materials/resources: who, what, and how with respect to the making of texts. In developing such curriculum we must also involve educators, community Elders, families, and students in the procedures for centring, infusing, integrating, and synthesizing curriculum changes and other relevant materials. An African-centred curriculum calls for a critical analysis of old and new texts/materials for omissions, biases, and exclusions of experiences around race, gender, sexuality, and difference. An African-centred curriculum must be available and easily accessible for students, educators, families, and community workers. In developing such curriculum, we combine school, wider community, and local cultural resource knowledge bases.

The promotion of "equity" and "excellence" through an African-centred educational philosophy requires searching for answers to some key challenges. First, African-centred education must be able to address the multiple needs and concerns of a diverse student body. The schooling community is never homogenous. Even in the African-centred school there are differences of class, gender, ethnicity, sexuality, [dis]ability, language, and religion. These differences must be acknowledged and responded to via the teaching, learning, and administration of education in the school. School curriculum, texts, classroom pedagogy, and the representation of teaching staff must also ensure that issues of diversity are front and centre of education. Learners must come out prepared to confront racism, sexism, homophobia, and other forms of systemic oppression. Second, African-centred education must ensure that excellence is not simply accessible but also equitable. This means there must be strategies that allow academically successful students to develop an obligation to other students facing difficulties. Success should be defined broadly and allow students to see their mutual obligations to each other. Examples include co-operative learning via the formation of study groups, pairing of students, and creation of classes with students of missed abilities. Third, African-centred educational philosophy must also ensure that all students are able to develop a sense of connectedness and identification to their schools. Strategies must aim to promote within students a sense of ownership for their own knowledge. Learning must be encouraged to develop students' leadership skills through adult-peer mentoring programmes. African-centred educational philosophy and approaches must foster ties between students, teachers, families, and homes to enhance youth learning. Fourth, African-centred educational strategy must move beyond the bland/seductive politics of inclusion to the pointed discourses of transparency and accountability. Measures to achieve these ends could include schools reporting to local communities and Elders, reaching out to the wider community, and developing chains of accountability beyond the official channels with school boards and education ministries. Engaging students to raise issues related to social responsibility, ones going beyond academic performance, we must help students to develop their sense of duty and citizenship. Excellence is also being enhanced broadly in such contexts as diverse students are able to define achievement beyond narrow preoccupations.

To achieve these ends African-centred educational approaches must develop effective methods for evaluating the appropriateness of classroom teaching materials/resources by addressing such questions as the who, what, and how regarding the making of texts and curriculum. The procedures for centring, infusing, integrating, and synthesizing curriculum and pedagogic changes and other relevant materials must situate the broad questions of equity and difference.

African-centred educational curriculum and teaching approaches must help challenge conventional and dominant notions of Blackness/Africanness. In mainstream North American society, Blackness has become synonymous with crime, excess deviancy, and underachievement. Among many Black youth there is the troubling sense of self-condemnation that is compounded by societal institutions, notably via education and the media. We need a psychic preservation of the self and the collective. African-centred educational philosophy promotes identity affirmation while challenging the dominant reading of Black[ness] as violent and subversive. African-centred educational approaches also provide counter-stories of Black and African successes, achievements, and resistance that help us challenge prevailing dominant narratives of Black masculinity. An important goal of African-centred schooling and education is to cultivate the ability of the learner to withstand the politically and culturally mediated experiences of conventional schooling through the development of a critical awareness and strong sense of self, values, purpose, and connectedness and belonging to a community of learners.

African-centred philosophical ideals are not simply for Black and African students. These are ideals that are shared by many Indigenous communities for their relevance to global humanism. For this reason, the African school is defined by its philosophical grounding rather than its racial characteristics. The school is defined more by its principles rather than by who goes or teaches in the school. Politically given that the school is intended to address issues of Black youth disengagement from mainstream school, it is hoped that the majority of students and teachers

3.2 The African-Centred Educational Philosophy as Anticolonial

in such a school will be of African descent. But the school and its ideas are not exclusionary to others.

An African-centred educational programme basically addresses programmatic issues to do with curriculum, pedagogy, and text. When a school programme integrates African-centred materials in the structures and processes of educational delivery, including teaching, learning, and administration of education, it can be argued that there exists an African-centred programme. Thus, such a programme may exist as one of many segments of a school. The distinguishing aspect between a "school" and a "programme" lies in the wholeness of education than an African-centred school promotes. In other words, an African-centred school is more than a textual, curriculum, or pedagogic consideration. It encompasses the following elements: the way the school is socially, politically, and culturally organized; how the schools' power relations are structured among students, educators, administrators, and local communities; the extent to which spirituality is integral to the conduct, culture, and value system of the school; the different ownership and responsibility roles for Elders, teachers, students, families, and the broader community.

In Dei et al. (2000) and Dei et al. (2002), we put forward seven domains for "inclusive education" that are equally relevant for an African-centred educational philosophy. These domains must be integrated and the absence of any one domain detracts from the power of the school. First, there is the issue of *representation*: (a) visual representation (representing Africa[nness] in the visual culture of schools); (b) knowledge representation (the active learning of African[a] cultures, histories, experiences, and knowledges); (c) physical representation (active recruitment, retention, and promotion of diverse physical bodies/staff, including African educators). Second, there is the question of *language* – promoting and enhancing local/Indigenous and first languages in schools. This educational approach views language as a mode of transmission of culture, history, identity, and ancestral knowledges. Language is seen as an embodiment of identity and political liberation, helping challenge learners to question and subvert the (dominant) language that minimizes, denigrates, and penalizes their experiences via the invalidation or a lack of comprehension of African cultural norms, values, and experiences. Third, there is the seeking out of *family and community partnerships* – creating spaces of knowledge and power-sharing for African family/community involvement in schools. Partnership areas include pedagogy, instruction, curriculum development, and community-school ties. This would include challenging the traditional practice of inserting families into already existing structures of schooling. Fourth, there is *co-operative education* – pursuing instructional and pedagogic practices that promote collective learning and responsibility by redefining "success" broadly to include academic and social achievements. Success should be seen as holistic, not simply the flip side of failure. Fifth, there is *equity, accommodation, and values education:* curricular approaches to address such forms of difference as race, gender, class, language, religion, disability, and sexuality to promote values that enhance the spiritual, emotional, and psychological development of the learner; and presenting teaching and learning as emotionally felt experiences. In this domain, education must emphasize the affective and psychomotor domains of the learner, not just cognitive competencies, including appreciation of love, justice, and spirituality. Sixth, there is the *Indigenous/community knowledges*. These are the ideas, norms, cultural knowledges, and common sense possessed by local peoples concerning their everyday realities of living. Such Indigenous knowledge would include the following: the use of "traditional knowledge" (i.e., using inter-generational knowledge of community Elders in schools); "*empirical knowledge*" (i.e., learners utilizing knowledge based on careful observations of their surrounding environments, homes, and communities); and revealed knowledge (using knowledges acquired through intuition, revelations, dreams, and visions). Seventh, the last aspect is *spirituality*. This is the educational philosophy that works with the concept of the learner as possessing a self, a personhood, and makes connections between the inner/outer space and environments. This is also about embodiment and embodied knowing. Spirituality in education is developing a cosmo-vision and embracing a critical humanism about interrelationships and connectedness, love and generosity for humanity, the interrelations of rights and responsibilities, the ties of the individual to community. It is also about the recognition of emotions, spiritual essence, and intuition as significant ways of knowing. Personal histories serve as sources of teaching and knowing.

Teaching and learning critically about Africa offers pedagogical possibilities for Black/African education in general. Among such possibilities are the urgency of addressing the issue of Black/African youth disengagement from school in Euro-American contexts, the problem of school dropouts or push-outs, and the low academic achievement by some youth (see also Brathwaite and James 1996; Codjoe 1997, 2001). Presenting knowledge about Africa seeks to nurture the self and the collective pride of youth in their identities and histories as African subjects, developing a sense of connectedness and identification with knowledge that can help improve upon learning outcomes. Education can be a tool for self and collective empowerment. In the next chapter, we consider one such pedagogical possibility, a new Pan-African social thought, as a space within which to model African ways of knowing and identities.

References

Asante, M. K. (1980) *Afrocentricity, the Theory of Social Change*. Buffalo: Amulefi Press.
Asante, M. K. (1990) *Kemet, African-Centredity and Knowledge*. Trenton, NJ: Africa World Press.
Asante, M. (1991a) The African-Centred Idea in Education. *Journal of Negro Education*, 60(2), 170–180.
Asante, M. K. (1991b) African American Studies: The Future of the Discipline. *The Black Scholar*, 22(3), 21–28.
Asante, M. K. (1992) African-Centred Curriculum. *Educational Leadership*. December 1991-January 1992, 28–31.
Bassey, M. O. (1999) *Western Education and Political Domination in Africa: A Study in Critical and Dialogical Pedagogy*. Westport, CT: Bergin & Garvey.
Brathwaite, K. and James, C. (Eds.) (1996) *Educating African Canadians*. Toronto: James Lorimer & Co.
Brock-Utne, B. (1996) Reliability and Validity in Qualitative Research Within Education in Africa. *International Review of Education*, 42(6), 605–621.

References

Brock-Utne, B. (2000) *Whose Education for All? The Recolonization of the African Mind.* New York: Falmer Press.

Cabral, A. (1970). National Liberation and Culture. *The 1970 Eduardo Mondlane Lecture*, Program of Eastern African Studies of the Maxwell School of Citizenship and Public Affairs, Syracuse University, February 20.

Codjoe, H. M. (1997). *Black Students and the School System: A Study of the Experiences of Academically Successful African-Canadian Student Graduates in Alberta's Secondary School.* Unpublished Ph.D. dissertation. Department of Educational Policy Studies, University of Alberta, Alberta, Canada.

Codjoe, H. (2001) Fighting a "Public Enemy" of Black Academic Achievement – The Persistence of Racism and the Schooling Experiences of Black Students in Canada. *Race, Ethnicity and Education*, 44, 343–376.

Dei, G. J. S. (1995) Examining the Case for African-Centred Schools in Ontario. *McGill Journal of Education*, 30(2), 179–198.

Dei, G. J. S. (1996a) *Anti-Racism Education in Theory and Practice.* Halifax: Fernwood Publishing.

Dei, G. J. S. (1996b) The Role of African-Centredity in the Inclusive Curriculum in Canadian Schools. *Canadian Journal of Education*, 21(2), 170–186.

Dei, G. J. S. (1997) Beware of False Dichotomies: Revisiting the Idea of "Black-Focused" Schools in Canadian Contexts. *Journal of Canadian Studies*, 31(4), 58–79.

Dei, G. S. (2004) Dealing with Difference: Ethnicity and Gender in the Context of Schooling in Ghana. *International Journal of Educational Development*, 24, 343–359.

Dei, G. J. S. (2007) Thinking and Responding to Difference: Pedagogical Challenges for African Education. In Mazama, A. and Asante, M. (Eds.) *Africa in the 21st Century*. Thousand Oaks, CA: Sage Publications.

Dei, G. J. S., I. M James, S. James-Wilson, L. Karumanchery, and J. Zine. (2000) *Removing the Margins: The Challenges and Possibilities of Inclusive Schooling.* Toronto: Canadian Scholar's Press.

Dei, G. J. S., C. James, E. Lawson, and M. Wood. (2005) *Towards Equitable Education for Black/African-Canadian Students in Ontario Schools.* Paper prepared for the Literacy and Numeracy Secretariat. Toronto: Ontario Ministry of Education.

Dei, G. J. S., S. James-Wilson, and J. Zine. (2002) *Inclusive Schooling: A Teacher's Companion to Removing the Margins.* Toronto: Canadian Scholar's Press.

Dei, G. J. S., J. Mazzuca, E. McIsaac, and J. Zine. (1997) *Reconstructing "Dropout": A Critical Ethnography of the Dynamics of Black Students' Disengagement from Schools.* Toronto: University of Toronto Press.

Dei, G. and Kempf, A. (Eds.) (2006) *Anti-Colonial Thought, Education and Politics of Resistance* (pp. 1–24). Rotterdam: Sense Publishers.

Du Bois, W. E. B. (1947) *The World and Africa.* New York: Viking Press.

Du Bois, W.E. B. (1969) *The Souls of Black Folk.* New York: Penguin. [Original Work published 1903].

Fanon, F. (1967) *Black Skin, White Masks.* NY: Grove Press.

Fanon, F. (1963) *The Wretched of the Earth.* New York: Grove Weidenfeld.

Foucault, M. (1980) *Power/Knowledge: Selected Interviews, 1972–77* Gordon, C. (Ed.). Brighton: Harvester Press.

Giroux, H. (1981) *Ideology and Culture and the Process of Schooling.* Philadelphia: Temple University Press.

Hilliard, A. (1992) Why We Must Pluralize the Curriculum. *Educational Leadership*, 49(4), 12–15.

Karenga, M. (1986) *Introduction to Black Studies.* Los Angeles: University of Sankore Press.

Karenga, M. (1988) Black Studies and the Problematic of Paradigm: The Philosophical Dimension. *Journal of Black Studies*, 18, 395–414.

Karenga, M. (2007). The Racial Reliability of Obama: An Unworthy and Contradictory Conversation. *Los Angeles Sentinel.* February 15, p. A9

Kempf, A. (Ed.) (2009) *Breaching the Colonial Contract: Anti-Colonialisms in the US and Canada*. Springer Press.

Konadu, K. (2006) The Current State of Black Nationalism. In Asante, M. and Mazama, A. (Eds.) *Encyclopaedia of Black Studies* (pp. 130–134). Thousand Oaks, CA: Sage Publishers.

Memmi, A. (1969) *The Colonizer and the Colonized*. Boston: Beacon Press.

Tajfel, H. (1981) *Human Groups and Social Categories: Studies in the Social Psychology*. London: Cambridge University Press.

Taylor, C. (1994) The Politics of Recognition. In Guttman, A. (Ed.), *Multiculturalism: Examining the Politics of Recognition* (pp. 25–74). Princeton: Princeton University Press.

Chapter 4
Theorizing Africa Beyond Its Boundaries

Abstract Resisting the localization of teaching Africa to the literal spaces of the Continent, this discussion traces theoretical and pragmatic ways – especially in our classrooms and political spaces – informal and formal African-centred learning and activism can happen.

Keywords Political activism · Teaching as resistance · Diversity of continental Africa · Local knowledges · Theory · Practice · Student engagement · Silenced histories · Teaching · Localization

4.1 Introduction

A trusted colleague recently asked me about the urgency to theorize Africa beyond its boundaries. On quick reaction, I thought this was quite evident given the diasporic connections and the rekindling of historic ties between African communities globally. This is an opportunity that cannot be lost. However, upon later reflection, I have come to realize that there must be far deeper and richer reasons why Africa must be seen beyond its geographical and spatial limits. I see a betrayal of the current generation and its high hopes for African unionism and the Pan-African vision of our foremothers and forefathers. I believe that there are social and intellectual responsibilities, ones held by the current generation of all scholars of African descent and students of Africa, to rethink what African and Africans stand for given that the stakes for continued division among African peoples are so high, as countries and peoples all over the world search for ways to create collective unions.

The promise of African peoples' liberation, the creation of Black African unity, and a New World Order respectful of political, economic, and cultural sovereignty of nations, as well as the mobilization of Southern nations to challenge Europe and the Western dominance, are great challenges confronting humanity. Imperialism, neocolonialism, and the "tentacles of the Empire" are far-reaching. Through the rhetoric of globalization a New World Order has emerged affirming the supremacy of Western values and ideals all under the guise of progress and development. There is a new name "globalization" or what Chinweizu (2006) calls, "the invasion of globalization rhetoric". It is what I call "imperial militocracy". This manifests itself not only in the ability of the West and Europe to act as "imperial saviours" but also to define the terms and rules of global engagement and to create new futures. In this undertaking Indigenous resistance to Western power is thwarted. Given the nature of globalization there is the need for political, cultural, and ideological spaces to challenge and resist these forces scripting the lives of African peoples.

Teaching about Africa today has implications for the conduct of the struggle of resistance to Western dominance. It is based on the belief in the power of ideas to bring about social change. I am speaking about knowledge that propels real change to disrupt white European supremacy. It is knowledge to foster the political, economic, and spiritual awareness of students of Africa. It is knowledge grounded in the realities of collective struggles for change by affirming destinies and ties to each other. It is a new wave of Pan-Africanism that extends the challenge beyond peoples of African descent to all students of Africa. Learning and teaching about Africa no longer becomes an exercise in the mere search for knowledge but the search to create, validate, and disseminate knowledge that would bring about social change in Africa. It is knowledge that compels political action.

The theory of Pan-Africanism is only meaningful if it is applied to the concrete problems and realities of African and oppressed peoples in the struggle for political, cultural, spiritual, social, and intellectual liberation. Peoples of African descent and students of Africa can no longer be satisfied with the current trend of becoming hyper-individualistic and hyper-nationalists. We need the teaching and learning of Africa to create knowledge that leads to a new brand of Pan-Africanism to reverse this course. This will be a Pan-Africanism that borrows from the ideas of old but adds new meanings and confronts challenges. It starts at the source of local community organizing by promoting a healthy approach to diagnosing current problems and offering African solutions. These will reflect an ideological frame and political approach not ashamed of our cultures, histories, and identities as peoples of African descent.

It is important to begin the debate on a new wave of Pan-Africanism by posing some questions. There is a tendency to view Pan-Africanism either as a history of often contradictory and opposing ideas; a chronology of events and historical figures or much more (Diawara 1996: 1). I believe asking new questions will move us in the right direction of critical thought and political action in addressing the challenges of Pan-Africanism and its relevance today in a global, transnational world. The questions I would like to pose include the following: How do we translate a pan-national and global idea of Pan-Africanism to the local level of communities? What can we make of the credibility of the African Union in the face of "ethnic cleansing" of Black Africans by Arab minority in the Darfur region of Sudan? Or the New Partnership for African Development (NEPAD), a vision and strategic framework for African renewal – by and for Africans – mandated by the Organization for African Unity in 2001, given that the budgets of African countries are still being approved in Washington? Quoting George Bush, who is the "decider"? Is the African Union "inside the dungeon of Western imperialism" (Chinweizu 2006)? Is NEPAD a centring of Western ideological interests as the basis for African development? What to do with neo-imperialist forces and internal colonialists (or again to use Chinweizu's characterization, the "Black comprador colonialists")? Where and what is the place of African Diasporian social thought (and realities) in the new Pan-Africanist ideology?

Notions of Nationalism, Pan-Africanism, and Socialism have all been essential and interrelated pillars and projects for liberation of oppressed people deeply rooted in African traditional values and culture. Together they serve as possibilities for organizing for change and search for genuine freedom. The basic objectives of Pan-Africanism include the following: self-determination of African peoples; independence from exploitative capitalist relations; the total liberation of all peoples of African descent; reclamation of African unity and strength and harnessing the synergies of African cultures and identities outside of the identity that is often constructed within Euro-American ideology/hegemony. There are significant African contributions to humanity. Thus, the scholarship and politics of Africans should first seek the intellectual wellness and improvement of the African person.

4.2 Re-conceptualizing Pan-Africanism Today

I define Pan-Africanism as social thought and practice linked to notions of culture, identity, freedom, and liberation to ensure and sustain sovereignty of African peoples and communities across diverse geographical spaces (borrowing from Konadu 2006: 130–134). This new Pan-African idea must be rooted in local understandings of political, cultural, and economic organizing, the cultivation of a Black spiritual consciousness, and the linking of individual and collective responsibilities to larger social causes. The idea is bigger than Africa and African peoples. Pan-Africanism must assert Africa's and African peoples' contributions to global humanity.

Pan-Africanism is also about a political, cultural, spiritual, and discursive challenge to the ideological hegemony and militarism of the Empire. Pan-African thought must be rooted in local, grassroots level social action and political activism. A re-conceptualized Pan-Africanism should foremost be about political education. If there is any failure of Pan-Africanism of old, it has to do with a "crisis of knowledge" about the lack of political sophistication to understand and tease out our own problems in the same vein as C.L.R. James (1977a, b), a Black nationalist, who saw the power of such education when talking about independence and revolutionary struggles in general.

The goal and objectives of a new wave of Pan-Africanism is the creation of African/Black power. The means to achieving this end is through African unity. It is important for us to know our ends in order to choose our means. Thus, I also conceptualize Pan-Africanism in the tradition of sharing in a "national culture" – the power of African culture and values – and "a return to the source" by going back to

African roots to develop a consciousness of existence as articulated by Amilcar Cabral (1980), Steve Biko (1979, 2002), and many others. The notion of Black African power as group power supersedes the individual nation power of African societies. It is power that can be utilized to achieve collective ends for all peoples of African descent as well as students of Africa. In this context, the preoccupation with "African unity" is only a means to an end, which is African power (Cabral 1980). The new wave of Pan-African thought and practice is about the social, cultural, and political rehabilitation of African communities globally.

In reflecting on the work of early thinkers of Pan-Africanism, going back to the nineteenth century, it is apparent that the ideas of the "integrationists" and "sovereignists" were both oppositional but also integrative. Edward Wilmot Blyden, born in the Virgin Islands in 1832 of African parents, came to the United States in 1850 to pursue education. He was denied admission because of his race. He migrated to Liberia and began arguing for African exodus from North America to found an independent African entity on the continent (Blake 2006: 244). His thinking was not to create an isolationist state but one determined to stand on its own and to link with the world on its own terms. Similarly, scholars such as Frederick Douglass, Martin Delany, and Sojourner Truth all had a vision of Black power. Delaney's *The North Star* publication called for Black political independence in Africa. Douglas and Truth further called for full citizenship for Blacks in the United States (see Delany 1993; Douglas 1969). While advocating an "Africa for Africans" on a visit to Liberia in 1859, Delany was mindful of an Africa that was part of a global community that had allies and sympathizers who respected African peoples for their long-cherished sovereignty and independence. Colonialism and enslavement had taken away such sovereignty, and it needed to be regained. Years later, when Booker T. Washington convinced Marcus Garvey to come to the United States, it was in the spirit of making connections between African and Black peoples elsewhere. Marcus Garvey's work with the "The United Negro Improvement Association" in Kingston, Jamaica, and later Harlem accorded him status. Viewed as the "father" of modern Black nationalism with his militant Pan-Africanist politics and "Back to Africa Movement", Garvey was borrowing from the intellectual ideas of others before him who had articulated African and Black peoples' sovereignty as well as political, economic, cultural, and spiritual independence. It is important to reiterate that the calls for the emergence of Black African power were only possible, if there was a consolidation of African interests in Africa, by Africans, and for Africans (Blake 2006).

Manning Marable (1995) notes that the perspective of Pan-Africanism was first advanced in the international context by barrister Henry Sylvester Williams of Trinidad and Tobago during the London conference of 1900. It was at this gathering that a young scholar, W.E.B. Du Bois (1969), predicted that the colour line would be the defining problem of the twentieth century. But there were significant subsequent events that were to define the history of Pan-Africanism. In 1945 in Manchester, England, W.E.B. Du Bois, George Padmore, Kwame Nkrumah, and other Black leaders from Africa, the Caribbean, Great Britain, and the United States held a major Pan-African conference aimed at strengthening ties of Black peoples across the Diaspora and to further the project of political liberation. A major demand at the conference was for Black Africa autonomy and independence.

One cannot offer a historical account of the genesis of Pan-African thought without referencing W.E.B. Du Bois. In his works *The World and Africa* and the classic *Souls of Black Folk*, Du Bois articulated four crucial points of interest to the Pan-African thesis and social movement. The first was that the history and culture of the people of Africa and African descent needed to be written as a necessary intellectual exercise. Second, the search for knowledge is valuable, if it allows Africans in the Diaspora to identify with the continent and to place Africa on an equal footing with Europe, Asia, and North America. In other words the necessity of developing an ontological lineage with Africa. Third, that it is important to posit "Africa's humanism and rich heritage as a compelling argument against racism and colonialism". Fourth, Black people everywhere would not be "completely free until Africa was liberated and emancipated in [anti-colonial] modernity". Later Malcolm X, Stokey Carmichael, Martin Luther King, and many others took up these causes. In fact, when Malcolm X visited Ghana in 1965, having met with President Nkrumah, he noted appreciably that they had "discussed the unity of Africa and peoples of African descent. We agreed that Pan-Africanism was the key also to the problems of [peoples] of African heritage" (Malcolm 1965: 410).

Kwame Nkrumah's Pan-Africanism was influenced by his mentor Marcus Garvey. Nkrumah credits "Philosophy and Opinions of Marcus Garvey" as very pivotal to his ideas. As a Garveyrite, Nkrumah's Pan-Africanism had both continental and global dimensions, particularly in his argument that the "affairs of Africa cannot be separated from the affairs of the world as a whole". Nkrumah realized early that Europe and the global community are implicit and implicated in the conquest, colonization, enslavement, and imperialist exploitation of Africa. Critical Pan-Africanist thought that failed to understand both the intellectual and political implications of this historic link was doomed to fail. Such understanding called for a politics of connecting struggles to the search for political solutions to global problems. Scholars have sought to distinguish between Garvey's "Black nationalism" and Nkrumah's "African nationalism", since there is a powerful intellectual connection between these two political ideologies. To Nkrumah the African continent was the cultural, political, and economic base of African peoples everywhere (Karenga 2007: 7).

Nkrumah incorporated Garvey's ideas and beliefs in the promise of Africa and Africans in human history. He reasoned accurately that the presuppositions and purposes of Western capitalism are contrary to African ideals given the history of plunder, oppression, devastation, and war that come with capitalist wealth. In effect, Nkrumah always perceived an external dimension to Africa's internal struggles and challenges as fundamental to Indigenous resolution of Black and African peoples' problems. It continues to this day in myriad forms.

The Canadian Broadcasting Corporation (CBC) radio ran a series on Ghana in connection with the 50th Anniversary Golden Jubilee celebration of independence from British rule. I was interviewed for an aspect on education. The segment on CBC was to my mind a very accurate account of those years post-Independence in Ghana. However, CBC did not mention the external dimensions of Ghana's current economic challenges. For example, the unfair international terms of trade that continue to plague African economies and serve to restrict much-needed foreign exchange resources were omitted from the accounting of problems. The CBC radio series put too much emphasis on corruption and not enough on external debt and trade imbalance. The impression that was left in the minds of listeners was that the reason for the lack of "development" was mostly internal.

Nkrumah's Pan-Africanism rested on the revolutionary potential or capacity of the masses to stir and nourish political consciousness. He espoused the idea of the "African Personality" as nurturing our culture and history to lead to a development of the African person while providing the intellectual and educational foundation of Pan-African future. Like some of the pioneer Pan-African thinkers Nkrumah enthused that as African peoples we look into our culture and history to represent the best of what it means to be African and human. It is for this reason that teaching African cultures and histories is so important to the youth of today, particularly African youth. In a world so consumed with material consumerism we need to teach youth to emphasize the human factor: the compassion and love for oneself and humankind, social responsibility, and service to a common cause and good. These teachings, touching upon the spiritual, sociocultural, and non-material components of development, may hold the key to Africa's eventual rebirth.

4.3 Historical Influences

Among the historical influences and antecedents to Pan-Africanism one can point to such developments as the African Liberation Struggles against enslavement, colonialism, and the search for emancipation. The Haitian American Revolution which inspired revolt by the working poor across ethnic and cultural lines was also influential in the development of the causes of the Pan-African struggles. There were the Citizenship and Civil rights struggles in the United States and the calls by African leaders for African Unity based on common causes of politics, economics, and cultural sovereignty. In this latter instance, the Organization of African Unity meeting in Addis Ababa in 1963 was critical. The Pan-African movement also influenced the cause and promotion of Black Education and African Studies in North America and Europe. For example, the Black Studies Movement was linked with the Pan-African Movement, inspiring African scholars and activists at Historically Black Colleges and Universities (HBCUs) to launch the Black Studies movement. Militant students, whether in Canada, the United States, or Britain, who asked for Black Studies were influenced by the Garvey movement and the Pan-African-congresses organized by Du-Bois. They also took inspiration from the African Liberation and African unity movements.

C.L.R. James called for "political intricacies" dictated by global events. He appropriated the "central themes of the French Revolution for Black liberation struggles and his repositioning of the Haitian uprising [1804] as the first paradigm of race unity between Black and Brown people in the modern world" (cited in Diawara 1996: 3). C.L.R. James discovered that Black unity "coincided with the quest

4.3 Historical Influences

for liberty, fraternity, and equality", the central themes of the French Revolution that Toussaint L'Ouverture appropriated for Haiti; of Aime Cesaire, who wrote *Discourse on Colonialism*; and of Frantz Fanon, who stated that "a nation which undertakes a liberation struggle rarely condones racism" (cited in Diawara 1996: 3).

The Negritude Movement spearheaded by Cesaire and Senghoir in their work on *The Black Noir* was influential to the Pan-African cause. The thesis of anti-racist racism contained in Jean-Paul Sartre's *Black Orpheus*, what has been termed the most famous essay on the Negritude movement, was an extension of the Negritude discourse (Sartre 1967). While celebrating both the Diopian and Leopald Senghor's "Negritude's racial essentialism" (Diawara 1996: 2), Sartre also embraced Marxism in the search for "a universal road beyond skin color" (Diawara 1996: 2). Sartre criticized the idea of "irreducible difference". He proposed a form of universalism that "the idea that Negritude is bigger even than Africa, that we were part of an international movement which held the promise of universal emancipation" (Diawara 1996: 5). Sartre's *Black Orpheus* was later criticized for diluting the meaning of Negritude and for "preventing the Black struggle from defining its own agenda for freedom and recognition" (Diawara 1996: 3). Sartrean views were criticized for universalizing "the Black struggle by positing Africa and other continents involved in the fight against colonialism and racism as the future of the world". The concern is that this approach changes "the goal of Negritude into something larger than the Black poets who invented it" (Diawara 1996: 4). It is worthy of note that Fanon, while coming out of the Negritude movement, later followed Sartre to declare the pitfalls of racial identification in *The Wretched of the Earth*, "when he argued that the unconditional affirmation of African culture has succeeded the unconditional affirmation of European culture" (Fanon 1968: 212). In many ways Fanon misread the way African culture was affirmed by the Negritude and later the Diopian thinkers. African culture was not valorized in a way to pillorize European culture. It was affirmed as legitimate in its own right and contrary to the devaluation of African culture and traditions by Europeans through Western education, Christianity, and "European civilization".

This is the position taken by the African-centred movement which called for a paradigm shift, centring African subjects in their own cultural frame of reference. Diopian theory has stressed the cultural unity of the people of African descent. It has called for a validation of what is African in contrast to the constant bombardment of the negativity of what Africa has stood for. The achievements and contributions of African peoples to world civilization are attested to in African-centred thought as a part of a critical consciousness of self and humanity by African peoples. Unfortunately, the Diopian or African-centred thesis has erroneously been essentializing race. Conversely, Diopian discourse uses racial consciousness as a social movement. Race is not and cannot simply be equated with politics. However, it is acknowledged by Diopian theorists that race, with all its fluidity and contextuality, still acts in broadly predictable ways and through well-rehearsed narratives to position Whites as superior to non-Whites, particularly Black and African peoples. The critique of skin colour as determinant of behaviour and character extends to the use of the colour descriptor for African peoples notwithstanding our diversity and richness of history and heritage. "Black" as a colour descriptor has become synonymous with crime, deviancy, violence, and subversion while "White" symbolises everything that is "good" about human society. White[ness] is usually juxtaposed with Black[ness]. In such problematic constructions of knowledge race offers entitlements and punishments.

The African-centred movement is a form of an intellectual reclamation and awakening. Steve Biko's (2002) concept of "Black consciousness" is useful in the development of critical thought about Africa and African/Black peoples. Such consciousness is a mental awareness and spiritual awakening of one's existence and knowledge of the oppressor/colonizer's conspiracy and threats to deny the humanity of the colonized and oppressed. It is the consciousness and courage to challenge the continued total subjugation of Black and African peoples. Similarly, Amilcar Cabral's (1980) notion of "national culture and liberation" stresses the importance of a people's culture that includes its knowledges, heritage, history, and the possibilities therein for revolutionary change.

4.4 Pedagogic Possibilities and Implications for Black/African Education

In discussing the pedagogic possibilities and implications of Pan-African thought for Black/African education, I want to raise three key issues of concern to the teaching and learning of and about Africa: (a) Reclaiming the Past, History, and Culture for Knowledge Production; (b) Possibilities of Anti-Colonial Education; and (c) Contesting and Engaging the Future through Unity and Community Building. These issues constitute the building blocks around which the broader politics of a new Pan-African social thought can be developed to achieve practical ends for teaching and learning about Africa and its peoples. There can be no proper engagement of Pan-African thought today without understanding what Africa's past, history, and culture offer for critical education. Similarly, as noted in the preceding chapter, any critical teaching and learning about Africa and its peoples must necessarily be "anti-colonial". Pan-African social thought is anti-colonial to the extent that it seeks to subvert the continued intellectual, economic, cultural, spiritual, and political subjugation and marginalization of Africa, its issues, and concerns in contemporary geo-politics. The way forward for Africa is building communities of solidarity and mutual regional partnerships that promote community and national development. This strength in unity would constitute the basis of an "African power" that some earlier Pan-African/anti-colonial thinkers advocated as the eventual goal of Pan-African politics. Consequently, the search for African unity only becomes a means to a larger end or goal.

First, on reclaiming the past, history, and culture for knowledge production, it is argued that the past and history are only meaningful if they offer lessons to guide the future. History has lessons to teach us. This is why educators must resist the temptation to amputate the present from the annals of our history. We cannot ignore the past irrespective of how pleasant or unpleasant that past is. Africa has a collective history. An awareness of such history shapes social thought processes. African's history of collective struggles against European colonization and enslavement constitute an important source of knowledge for the development of a critical social thought about resistance, survival, and what it means to have a sense of community and common purpose. But history is equally about unity, disunity, and tensions. Teaching such complex histories creates an understanding of the contradictions of human existence, its possibilities, and its challenges as we strive for collective survival. History and its knowledge cannot be ignored. Condemning history to the trash bin is a curse and a Recipe for disaster.

In a thought-provoking paper, Seixas (2002) notes that there is an intense interest in history that has emerged with a growing or heightened historical consciousness. History is ongoing with signs of continuity and change. History is multilayered and complex. History is itself influenced by context and locations. Our historical interpretations rest on social and political relationships and forces. Subordinate groups who in the past have had their histories told or defined for them by the dominant are now insisting on reclamation of these histories. They are insisting on re-telling their stories and histories from different vantage points. These developments, as Seixas (2002) notes, have "forced a re-examination of the stories of the past" (3). History has thus become an anchor of shared and competing values as well as an intense outlook of the past. Histories reinforce collective identities, social vales, and moral and cultural orientations. Yet no history is irrelevant. Historical accounts must help provide all learners with social meanings to events and social causes. There may be differing and conflicting accounts of history with various meanings and interpretations of the past. Historical accounts are often contradictory depending on who the narrator is and/or who constructs knowledge as history. Given the complexity of history, it is important for us to understand the "distance between the present and the past, and the difficulty of representing the past in the present" (Seixas 2002: 4). This is not to say that the past is irrelevant. The "pastness of the past" means we must exercise intellectual caution and care when it is reclaimed to serve or explain contemporary causes. Our task as critical educators is to present these varied accounts and contestations of history – the points and counterpoints, the divergent stories – to students and help them come to a fuller understanding or appreciation of the contradictions and conflicts. This is one important way students of history can reach "a robust historical judgment". We must teach history via its complexities, with its multiple causes and consequences, and to draw on its powerful lessons that all too often have been rendered "irrelevant". We must offer our students a deep understanding of the past, present, and the future continuum.

In teaching and learning African history and its past, we are bringing critical knowledge about a people to the learner. Such history must be taught from the vantage point of Indigenous/local peoples as creators of their own destiny. Local peoples cannot be seen as lacking agency. They are not passive recipients of knowledge.

They have influenced the course of history themselves and have been active players in the events around them that have shaped and continue to shape their futures.

African history teaches about struggles and resistance. It teaches about achievements, failures, and contributions to the global scene. It teaches about the ways communities function: to come together to carve out a future from the "ruins" of enslavement and colonization, incorporate their economies into global capital and market forces, and form sites of resistance and strength.

Africa has long been a source of important knowledge for the development of the discipline. African sources of data have shaped the formulation of theories in political science, sociology, anthropology, and other social science disciplines. In pursuit of such knowledge, Africa has at times been subjected to a form of intellectual aggression where researchers claim expertise on African affairs some times with just cursory or partial knowledge of African peoples, cultures, and histories. In teaching Africa, it is important that the claim to know Africa and her peoples must be embodied such that students can bring a political and cultural consciousness and emotional attachment to knowledge.

Reclaiming history is also reclaiming culture and rootedness in place and context. African cultures are vibrant, rich, and diverse. They constitute important teachings about the society-nature nexus. Culture is an embodiment of a people's social wealth. It includes the material and concrete manifestations of everyday social life, as well as the non-material aspects which include the norms, values, and mental constructs of a people. A groundedness and affirmation of culture is to root people in history, place, and time. It is also to acknowledge a richness and depth in history. No culture is static or frozen in time and space. Culture is an ongoing process. The teachings of African cultures must proceed in ways that show the dynamism and interplay of cultures and traditions. Critical teaching also requires that students of Africa be exposed to the sites and sources of culture that can empower as well as disempower people. We know that there are some aspects of African cultures that can place women, the poor, youth, ethnic, sexual, religious, linguistic minorities, and people with disabilities in disadvantageous positions. African culture and tradition, while privileging certain core values, may also infringe on rights and freedoms of peoples. Consequently, no tradition is immune to criticism. But we cannot engage in a wholesale denigration of African culture and tradition.

Culture remains a site of continual struggle. In fact, culture everywhere is contested. It is political and can be politicized for particular ends and purposes. There are power-related issues of culture as reflected in gender, class, ethnicity, sexuality, and age differences in the affirmation of cultures. It is important that the teaching of African culture emphasize these contestations and the nature of power differences and their effects of communities.

African development is not simply a matter of economic, technological, and material "advancement". It is equally about cultural, spiritual, and social development of a people. Development must draw on the links between body, mind, spirit, and soul, as it seeks a combination of the culture, society, economics, politics, science, and technology. The new Pan-African social thought is about a cultural rebirth, a reclaiming of culture in its complexities and tensions for positive (solution-oriented) ends. A rootedness in African culture creates a social awareness of the tensions, struggles, and contradictions of everyday life and history. The recourse to history is to draw on the important and valuable lessons to guide the present and future.

4.5 The Possibilities of Anti-colonial Education

The anti-colonial thesis argues that colonialism is unending. This thesis crucially reframes Pan-African social thought for contemporary times. Anti-colonial education should be about intellectual and political vigilance. Responding to the challenges of "neo-colonial brainwashing" (Chinweizu 2006) that downplay what Africa and peoples of African descent have to offer the world, the unconditional affirmation of everything from the West by segments of local populations/communities is a legacy of European colonialism and imperialism. We have been taught to devalue everything Indigenous and African. In some contexts Africa and what African peoples have to offer play secondary roles to Europe and Western interests. There is a craving for material possessions of the West. Capitalist consumerism has led to the commodification of Indigenous cultures. Anti-colonial education is to subvert colonial hierarchies and colonizing relations reproduced in ethnic, class, gender, sexual, age, and intergenerational relations.

Anti-colonial education re-theorizes the link between education and development. While education is important for national development, it is the nature, content, and form of education that are fundamentally critical to promoting genuine development. Relevant education must be anchored in local peoples' aspirations, Indigenous cultures and values, and tailored foremost to meet local needs and concerns. This form of education has a better chance of promoting collective social development. Anti-colonial education seeks the following: connections with local communities' knowledge; cultivating in learners a deep sense of personal, social, and collective responsibility; a sense of obligation to oneself, peers, and community; building mutual interdependence and trust with others by subverting power hierarchies. In anti-colonial education the question of the relevance is equally critical – the educational relevance of the school curriculum, texts, classroom pedagogy, and instruction. Anti-colonialism seeks answers to such questions as the following: What are students learning? How appropriate is the knowledge to their local conditions? How does the knowledge help them solve problems and challenges of everyday living? How does such knowledge prepare students to engage the outside: regional, national, and global communities? How does this education prepare the youth for a future of self and collective actualization of dreams? How does the education help the learner to know and understand their environments, social conditions, and present social engagements? It is important that school curriculum and classroom teaching be Indigenized to local communities and create a "community of learners".

Anti-colonial education is also about affirming African identities. Knowing the self, relations with peers and others, and one's place in the larger realm of things are important. Education that seeks to build the self and collective identity of learners supports students as they achieve. Education must begin with knowing the self as an important entry point to knowledge production. Anti-colonial education in this context also engages the question of what it means to be African or a person of African descent and the responsibilities that come with such knowing. Producing knowledge about Africa should present Africa in a positive light to counter the negative images and portrayals of the continent and its peoples. It does not mean we gloss over the disparities and inequities in society. In fact, such knowledge should present a comprehensive picture. However, there is a special obligation on the part of the student of Africa to be equipped with knowledge that helps counter all the falsehoods spread about Africa and its peoples. Teaching and learning Africa must be about its contributions to humanity and global civilization.

As alluded to in a previous chapter, anti-colonial education is also a rethinking of the post-colonial education project of national integration, citizenship responsibility, and nation building. While the goals of education are to promote social cohesion and integration, these cannot be pursued by downplaying differences and the inequities that exist along the lines of gender, class, ethnic, religious, and linguistic differences in schooling (Dei et al. 2006). Anti-colonial education works with difference by emphasizing the strength in diversity and difference; it affirms how the "unity in sameness" connects to "unity in difference". By addressing the asymmetrical relations of power structured along difference, schooling and education can openly subvert colonial and colonizing relations as they play out in schools and the wider society.

In effect, the pedagogic implications of Pan-African social thought – how we teach and model – call for a critique of attempts to decouple scholarship from politics. Education and producing knowledge about Africa should be relevant for African causes. Education cannot be knowledge for its own sake. Anti-colonial education is political education. It seeks to subvert colonial and colonizing hierarchies and dismantle social inequities. One cannot fight social inequity without engaging in politics. There must be room for the politics of education that is not prescriptive. Those who pursue education to the contrary have legitimate grounds to claim they are apolitical. Such claims are political in the first place as they seek to protect the status quo.

4.6 Contesting and Engaging the Future Through Unity and Community Building

Africa can achieve a status of "super power" through community building and mutual economic, cultural, political, and spiritual partnerships with other communities. Black/African Power is what would accord respect to African peoples on the global stage. It is a Pan-African ideal, one wherein Africa comes first. We need a promotion of ideals and knowledge that will ensure that such power can be achieved by the continent and all peoples of African descent. Pan-African ideology employs notions of "community" and "communities of difference". It implies a "unity in sameness" as well as "unity in difference". Africa and its peoples constitute very diverse communities. There are differences among communities, regions, and nations. Underneath these differences, African peoples share a collective history of struggle against enslavement, colonialism, imperialism, and the encroachment of global market forces. The ways in which these forces play out in communities may differ from region to region, nation to nation, but we must be able to see a common destiny beyond these differences. These differences must be harnessed as sites of strength by connecting links among nations and communities. In order to move ahead Africa needs to forge ties among its communities and nations. A "Unity of Nations" – an African Union – with strong leadership having the foresight and a defined vision, mandated with a clear sense of purpose, can be a strong force. It can be supported by the vast natural and human resources of the continent so that a truly African agenda is not dictated to by external forces. This Union can and should seek to unite Indigenous solutions to Africa's problems. It can take its lead by resolving internal disputes and promoting genuine African development through regional solidarities, especially via regionalism. Diasporic communities have a role to play in this regards. This is where a theorization of Africa beyond its boundaries becomes critical. By stressing bonds that link African communities through history, we are able to make diasporic and continental connections. A new Pan-African ideology must connect issues: the ways race, ethnicity, gender, sexuality, disability, and patriarchy play out in communities' social relations; how questions of health, environmental sustainability, economics, and poverty are deeply interrelated in the quest for genuine development options for Africa and African peoples; and how to secure and preserve local knowledges with non-African insights.

A good starting point to teach critically about Africa is to examine the notion of "African development". The next chapter, in considering some of the intellectual pitfalls within the "development" discourse, also examines how the practice of "teaching Africa" opens possibilities for change and alternatives.

References

Biko, S. (1979) *Black Consciousness in South Africa*. Arnold, M. (Ed.). New York: Vintage.
Biko, S. (2002) *I Write What I Like: Selected Writings*. Chicago: University of Chicago Press.
Blake, C. (2006) An African Nationalist Ideology in Diaspora and the Development Quagmire: Political Implications. In Asante, M. and Karenga, M. (Eds.) *Handbook of Black Studies* (pp. 243–258). Thousand Oaks, CA: Sage Publishers.
Cabral, A. (1980) *Unity and Struggle*. Wolfers, M. (trans.). London: Heinemann Educational Books.
Chinweizu. (2006). *An Achebe Foundation Interview with Paul Odili*. Lagos, Nigeria, September 3, 2006. File://C:\Documents%20and%20Settings.
Dei, G. J. S., Asgharzadeh, A., Eblaghie-Bahador, S. and Shahjahan, R. (2006) *Schooling and Difference in Africa: Democratic Challenges in a Contemporary Context*. Toronto: University of Toronto Press.
Delany, M. R. (1993) *The Condition, Elevation, Emigration and Destiny of Coloured People of the United States*. Baltimore: Black Classic.

Diawara, M. (1996). Pan-Africanism and Pedagogy. http://www.blackculturalstudies.org/m_diawar/panafr.html
Douglas, F. (1969) *My Bondage and My Freedom*. New York: Arno Press.
Du Bois, W. E. B. (1969) *The Souls of Black Folk*. New York: Penguin.
Fanon, F. (1968) *The Wretched of the Earth*, tr. Constance Farrington. New York: Grove.
James, C. L. R. (1977a) *Nkrumah and the Ghana Revolution*. Westport: L. Hill.
James, C. L. R. (1977b) *The Future in the Present: Selected Writings*. London: Allison and Busby.
Karenga, M. (2007). Speaking Freedom, Celebrating The People: Ghana @50, Nkrumah @First. *Los Angeles Sentinel* (March 8), p. A7.
Konadu, K. (2006) The Current State of Black Nationalism. In Asante, M. and Mazama, A. (Eds.) *Encyclopaedia of Black Studies* (pp. 130–134). Thousand Oaks, CA: Sage Publishers.
Malcolm, X. (1965) *The Autobiography of Malcolm X: As Told to Alex Haley*. New York: The Random House Publishing Group.
Marable, M. (1995). "Pan-Africanism: Yesterday and Today" Along the Colour Line. November 1995. http://afgen.com/pan-afri.html
Padmore, G. (n. d.). Padmore's Question: Pan-Africanism or Communism? http://www.etext.org/Politics/MIM/countries/panafrican/padmore/pademorereview.html
Sartre, J. -P., Black Orpheus, tr. John MacCombie. (1967) *What is Literataure? and Other Essays*. Cambridge, MA: Harvard University Press.
Seixas, P. (2002) The Purposes of Teaching Canadian History. *Canadian Social Studies*, 36(2).

Chapter 5
Teaching Africa: "Development" and Decolonization

Abstract Challenging the pervasive position of the Western expert – the Africanist – as a long-standing literal and metaphoric figure, this discussion invites readers to transcend this power relationship. The chapter attempts to reframe the power dynamics by inviting the reader to consider development as an African-centred process of coming to power, knowledge, and identity.

Keywords Challenging the Africanist · Knowledge formation · Teaching · Power dynamics · Claiming power · African knowledges · Indigeneity · Development · Decolonization · Identity formation

5.1 Introduction

In recent years we have witnessed a surge in the literature on the social, political, economic, and knowledge critiques of what has constituted conventional "development". I will utilize Vincent Tucker's (1999) re-conceptualization of "development" for my approach to re-theorize the development concept for teaching about Africa. Moreover, I will draw insights from Zaiadinn Sardar's (1999) nuanced critique of the dominance of Eurocentricity. Sardar's informative work fits into both my intellectual and political project of reframing development for teaching about Africa.

Any critical engagement with the concept of development requires deconstruction. However, as Linda Smith (1999) reminds us, it is important to bear in mind that it is not enough to deconstruct, one must decolonize at the same time. Deconstruction without decolonization within the context of critical anti-colonial work has only limited potential for transformation; this work also carries the potential to reproduce the very asymmetrical power relations that one is seeking to transform, rupture, and overturn. I say this given that decolonization questions the paradigms through which we view ourselves individually/collectively, our place in the world, and our vision of that world, and our past, present, and future.

How we see the paradigms that we use determines the questions we ask. These questions must be posed as critiques. Without a decolonizing framework as a foundational basis, we cannot challenge colonial world views. Both Sadar (1999) and Tucker (1999) point to the pitfalls of "Teaching Africa" while looking at their reconceptualization of the concept of "development". The foundational premise, from which this critical study begins, lies in acknowledging the sociocultural locations from which the world is viewed. The Eurocentric standpoint is conceptualized and problematized not simply in curricular forms or in terms of ethnocentric bias, but as a hegemonic and pervasive world view. The foundational process of "Teaching Africa" necessitates a critical engagement with "development" as discourse and the oppressive relations therein. "Teaching Africa" must be pursued in relation to a collective experience of African Indigenity. The reference to Indigenity highlights the local/Indigenous knowledge of African peoples as significant for re-theorizing, reframing, and promoting development. The local cultural resource knowledges of African peoples have not been analysed for their contributions to the African development process. Any critique of the "problem" of African development, especially in a project of critically Teaching Africa, must acknowledge this omission while bringing to the discursive carpet the dominance of Eurocentric framings on issues of and about Africa and African peoples.

5.2 The Problem with "African Development"

"Teaching Africa" necessitates an interrogation of the dominant Western conceptualization of Africa, one produced and reproduced within and through European Enlightenment ways of thought. Such ways of thinking have been promulgated by scholars such as Diderot, Hegel, and Kant. Africa is constructed as a fixed and homogenized ethnocultural body residing at the bottom of an imagined hierarchical racial scale of human evolution with Europeans positioned at the very top. There also needs to be a recognition of critical consciousness, notably Freire's (1970: 74) notion of *conscientization*, that is to say, the process of "learning to perceive social, political, and economic contradictions, and to take action against the oppressive elements of reality." Here the Freirian anti-colonial conceptualization of *contradictions* reflects and is integral to Fanon's (1967) notion of demystification.

Crucial to the process of decolonization, demystification entails an exerted challenge of the colonial discourse that enforces the notion that universal knowledge of the colonizer is superior to that of the colonized. Demystification reveals how colonial domination is mediated through and within Eurocentricity. Demystificaton takes up an interrogation of "obscuring language" (Fanon 1967: 189) that serves to mask the violence of ongoing colonial relations of power mediated through contradiction. For example, Frantz Fanon points out that through interrogation and deconstruction "function... the main laws of [colonial] economics" (1967: 190). People come to understand that "wealth is not the fruit of labor but the result of organized, protected robbery" (1967: 191). Demystification reproduces and maintains social

5.2 The Problem with "African Development"

relations designed to leave African peoples in a material and psychological state of subjugation and dependency in relation to the West.

Demystification in the context of decolonization and a contestation of Eurocentricity entails learning to become conscious of the violence of contradiction. Demystification necessitates that learning becomes conscious of the contradiction of the promise of colonialism. While colonization promised "development", it delivered systems of oppression and dependence for Indigenous peoples. Walter Rodney (1972) and the scholars of developed theory pinpointed the violent disjunction between what capitalist colonial discourse promised versus the material reality for African peoples.

Capitalist colonialism promised prosperity and high standards of living; in reality, however, it created starvation, poverty, and daily misery. Capitalism and imperialism promised greater health and well-being through what they considered superior forms of technologies, ideas, and knowledges; instead, they created decreases in life expectancy, rising infant mortality rates, and increases in diseases such as diphtheria (Rodney 1972: 237; Ake 1982: 84–85). Colonialism was justified "on the grounds that it was to the mutual advantage of the colonizer and the colonized" (Ake 1982: 83). Promising new agararian technologies and greater food production, colonialism actually increased starvation and malnutrition. It promised schooling and education but in reality delivered an education system that served to psychologically wound, despiritualize, and alienate African children from any sense of collective Indigenous self. Claude Ake (1982: 84) further points out that this material and epistemic brutalization stood "in harmony with its claims" and logic. Rodney perceived that the contradictions of Eurocentric colonial discourse necessitated that colonialism was not merely a system of exploitation but one where "the essential purpose was to repatriate profits back to the so called mother country through the 'consistent expatriation of surplus' [wealth] produced by African labour out of African resources" (Rodney 1972: 149). Critical consciousness happens as one becomes conscious of this process and aware of the politics of contradiction. These elements are integral to what defines demystification: becoming aware of how Eurocentric promises result of oppressive colonial structures.

Ania Loomba (1998), writing in her analysis of the Oxford English Dictionary's definition of "colonialism", notes that it refers to notions of settlement and the forming of a community in a "new locality" by a body of peoples; however, it "avoids any reference to people other than the colonizers". That people might have already been living in the "new locality" is erased. The implication of subjugation, domination, and dispossession of an existing people are eschewed. As Loomba (1998: 1–2) explains, the definition "evacuates the word colonialism of any implication of a [violent] encounter between peoples or of conquest and domination". The definition evacuates the reality that the process of forming a community necessitates the violence of *unforming* a community. It erases epistemic violence.

The concept of "development" is defined and conceptualized in ways that produce similar evacuations. Let us consider the following definition of "development": "development is a standard borne by those who would promote the interests of the affluent and the powerful as well as by those who would serve the non-affluent and the unpowerful: by those who would expand the reach of the most industrialized states and those who would shield the least –modernized from nefarious influences; by those who would stress the virtues of entrepreneurship and individualism and those who would nurture community and collective concerns; by those who would pursue strategies of top-down initiative and decision-making and those who advocate a bottom-up, or grass-roots, approach" (Black 1991: 15). This definition is problematic as it fails to acknowledge profound contradictions in the development discourse. It can also be critiqued for how Eurocentrism fails to acknowledge the historical and cultural values embedded in the concept of development, especially the power relations upon which it rests. Let us consider some of these critiques.

5.3 Development as Eurocentric Paradigmatic Way of Knowing

What I am calling for here is an engagement with alternative frameworks of knowing that stand in opposition to the discursive and material practices of Eurocentricism and conventional "development". This discussion will require an unpacking of Eurocentricity and its implication in the discourses of "development", as well as the ways in which development is taken up in African contexts. Language and discourse are critical here. I am also thinking of Foucault's (1972) archaeology of knowledge – the archive is a cultural library of statements, ideas, and discourses that limit what can be said. The implication is that African scholars may be constrained in determining the "challenges" faced by schooling in African contexts. On an epistemic level it is crucial to note that the evacuations are produced and reside within the consciousness. wa Thiongo (1986) asks us to decolonize the mind and unpack the concept of development.

As Vincent Tucker (1999: 2) rightly argues, "development" is not a universal concept nor can it be translated in transnational contexts as if it were a universal given. Rather, it is an explicitly cultural entity produced within a Eurocentric colonial discursive framework of thought and material practice in which mythology and imagination play key roles in its hegemonic reproduction. The concept of development is "elevated to the status of natural law, objective reality and evolutionary necessity. In the process all other world views are devalued and dismissed as 'primitive' 'backward', 'irrational' or 'naïve'" (Tucker 1999: 2). The myth of development and its hegemonic power stem in part from the notion that development is simply a natural universal process. The concept of development is evacuated, to borrow Mama's (1995) description and reference to notions of evolutionary progress, of historical context. A key evacuation that furthers the myth of development lies in the Enlightenment discourse and its process of Otherization.

The re/production of the myth of development is dependant on the decoupling of this myth from reality, a separating of critical knowledge from Western identity formations. Development is not simply a concept. It is a Western discourse and the outcome of a hegemonic process that has violent material consequences. It is a colonial and imperial discourse. As Tucker (1999) argues "[d]evelopment ....is the process whereby other peoples are dominated and their destinies are shaped according to an essentially Western way of conceiving and perceiving the world. The development discourse is part of an imperial process" (Tucker 1999: 2). The evacuation of these historical contexts, languages, and discourses serves to produce "development as Eurocentric discourse whose re/production depends upon its re/production as an imagined entity" (Tucker 1999: 2).

To argue "development" is a Eurocentric discourse is a huge undertaking and not without risks. The so-called development discourse is filled with myths that need to be contested via an intellectual politics of demystification: the coming to consciousness that development as discourse is not simply a set of statements and ideas that are "out there" in texts but that they hold powerful sway and implicate bodies significantly (see also Munck 1999). Tucker (1999: 16–17) contends "people inhabit them" as part of a political act of identification. Ziauddi Sardar (1999) also explains that "the real power of the West does not lie in its 'economic muscle' nor its 'technological might' but rather in its 'power to define'" (Escobar 1994). A crucial aspect of conceptualizing "Teaching Africa" then is to engage in a process of conscientization. This moves into the constraining of the power of Eurocentricity (in relation to development and scholarly analysis of Africa) to define what is worth knowing about Africa. The question of what is the prism/lens through which Africa has been understood and interpreted is relevant to the discussion. Such interpretations of Africa have come through particular lenses, ones often misinformed or refracted through others' experiences with African peoples' knowings that are usually dismissed or undervalued. Given that the power of Eurocentricity to define is at heart of the development crisis or dilemma, as far as African development is concerned, then how Africa has conventionally been read and understood cannot be underemphasized. We need to step outside of the archive of dominant knowledge to be able to conceptualize development differently for Africa.

5.4 Teaching Africa: Chabal and the Power of Eurocentricity

What is implied in a discussion of the 'nature of the present African "crisis?" I refer to Chabal (1996) because his conceptual analysis and discursive framework provide us with a critical reflection of the structural implications of Eurocentricity in its power to constrain thought, imagination, and conceptual possibilities. Chabal (1996) rightly speaks of "three broad frameworks for interpreting 'postcolonial African politics'". Chabal points to a weakness of Eurocentric thinking about Africa that sees the continent in periodic phases and in the aftermath of a colonial process. The colonial is being re-organized while it endures. But let us leave this for a moment. Examining his conceptualization of personal locatedness, Chabal's work reveals the "specific analytical difficulties" Africanists face. There are what he calls the "politics of the mirror", "the tyranny of causalities" and "the implications of enunciation" (1986: 45). It is the politics of the mirror and the implications of enunciation that I want to take up here.

The ways in which European Africanists have historically and contemporarily viewed Africa are as exoticized "counterpoints" to a European historical standpoint, imagined in the Hegelian Enlightenment mode of history, rationality, reason, and the Cartesian separation of mind and body. From this standpoint the Africanist anthropologist then looks for "primitive societies from which we [read White Europeans] are supposed to have evolved" (Chabal 1996: 45). Explorers and missionaries, including the charities and selected non-governmental organizations of the secular neo-missionary variety, have continually observed Africa through "their perspective of the evolution of their own Western societies". There is an "imagined lens, an imagined construction of 'backwardness' of the African continent [and of African Peoples] in relation to the *development* [my italics] of the West". Chabal's understanding of the politics of the mirror and its effects reveal "an image of the African that would confirm *our* developmental assumptions about *ourselves*" (45, emphasis added).

Chabal (1996) identifies the process of otherization in historical Africanist thinking following the works of Fanon and Said. The Other – the African and the Oriental – emerges, is produced, and reproduced as an invention of the West, of Europeaness, and of the Occident. This Othering serves as means through which the dominant can locate itself. Chabal's (1996) concern lies in the extent to which identities and politics of the mirror in historical contexts influence contemporary thought processes and analyses of Africanists. Chabal (1996: 46) asks how the "Caliban syndrome" dictates Africanist perceptions "of the conditions and needs of Africa".[1] Such perceptions are manifested in and through an ongoing conceptual framework which determines that "when Africans speak *we* only hear what comforts the notion of Africa *we* hold and the extent to which Africans have learnt to speak the language *we* want or need to hear." This framework is determined by a tribalist paradigm of primitive communities, essentialized and fixed in the early stages of human evolution, giving rise to what Chabal calls the "tyranny of causalities". The "politics of a mirror" influences the analysis of issues in contemporary Africa in terms of "causalities". Interpreting "complex processes in Africa [is done] by way of simple causalities which *we* would never accept in respect of *our* own societies" (47). According to Chabal (1996: 45–46), the main framework of Africanist analysis of postcolonial African politics

> stems from both Development theory – an all conquering theory of causal explanations dating from European imperialist/colonializing theories of evolution and whereby development/underdevelopment ... position African peoples in social and cultural terms perceived as being close or at the bottom of the evolutionary scale – and in terms of economic development – occupying a position just above hunting and gathering societies but well below feudal ones – which in turn justified colonial domination.

---

[1] Caliban, a character from William Shakespeare's *The Tempest*, derives his name from an anagram of cannibal. The term cannibal alludes to Christopher Columbus' reference to the Cannibals or Caribes. Caliban is presented as a part-human and part-monster amalgam. His racialized heritage renders him uncivilized.

The development theorists, according to Chabal (1996: 47, 49), start out from preconceived notions of tribalism. They are informed by notions of ethnicity conceptualized in African contexts as "a condition which afflicts the 'other' at an early stage in evolution". The tribal/ethnicity perspective is not the fault of African peoples. Ethnicity is interpreted as "left over from previous [primitive age]" or a "false consciousness which afflicts [African] peoples [who are] easily misled by ruthless leaders". The key point that Chabal is making here is that the "politics of the mirror" is implicated in what "we" can or cannot say.

Chabal still conceives Africa and African peoples through a "tribal" paradigm where power relations along the lines of social difference that impact and inform "our" societies' and "theirs" are not viewed as being in need of decolonization. Similarly, there is no critique of the notion of "our" society and the dialectical relationship of power existing between the global North and South, no awareness of the need for a decolonization of Europe, and no need to race Europe itself. In fact, the very notion of an "Africanist" calls for self-interrogation by Chabal as a critical starting point.

Critical voice, as conceptualized by Chabal (1996: 50), is framed as the voice and analytical self of the "we", the search for universal concepts, and a "vocabulary which will make it possible to advance insight into the realities of contemporary Africa". Chabal uses this framework to call for the Indigenous languages in which Africans themselves express their understanding of politics (51).

Where is decolonization? There is a critical discursive weakness that can be identified as the source of the problem which is a crucial and integral component of "teaching Africa". The central problem lies in a disavowal of any complex interrogation of self as being implicated as a product or carrier of Eurocentrism. What we understand by the notion of "knowledge[s]" is also crucial here. Chabal never asks the question, preferring Eurocentric conceptual frameworks to interpret African ways of doing. As Sadar has rightly argued, "the problem of Eurocentrism, and hence the problem with development, is thus the problem of knowledge. It is a problem of discovering Other ways of knowing, being and doing. It is a problem of how to be human in ways Other than those of Europe. It is also a problem of how the West could liberate its true self from its own colonial history and moorings" (60).

5.5 Afrocentrism in – and Is – Us

Fanon (1967) pinpointed the psychic destructiveness of internalization of Eurocentrism through his analyses of colonialism and colonization. In the African context, wa Thiong's (1986) work points to the social death of community, the carrier of culture, language, and paradigmatic ways of knowing. wa Thiongo, in rejecting the English language, was fully aware of the fact that knowing one's past and the cultural knowledges that define who one is are important.

The past and local cultural knowings are intertwined. A lack of rootedness in the past, culture, and tradition is itself an abrogation of an important knowing. When we replace other ways of knowing with a dominant perspective that denigrates or devalues other experiences and knowledge, it constitutes a serious intellectual problem. This has been a critique offered against Eurocentricity in its power to devalue other ways and to masquerade as the only legitimate way of knowing. Colonial education in Africa contributed to the process of devaluing African ways of knowing, further sowing the seeds of Eurocentricty in the African learner.

But the power of Eurocentricty is much more. Sardar (1999) makes a critical point in relation to Eurocentricity: it defines the past, present, and future (Sardar 1999: 60). The internalization of Eurocentrism only shows that "the West is in us" (Sardar 1999). This becomes crucial in the contexts of African scholarship and African discursive analysis of the "challenges" that confront African academies. These include the conceptualization of " African crisis" and the framing of African schooling in the present and, more importantly, the future. As African learners, we all continually struggle to break away from an imposed Eurocentric lens and cultural framings.

Abagi (2005), for example, shows the conceptualization of schooling in African contexts as it relates to the internalization of Eurocentricsm. Referring to the role of schooling in Africa in the twenty-first century, Abagi (2005) characterizes this era as one for "coping with change". Abagi states his position by quoting Ocitti's (1973) reference to the imperatives for African schooling. Occiti makes the point that it is crucial to "develop or move away from the narrow conventional concept of education as schooling to the more acceptable and realistic Indigenous conceptualization of education". This stresses "the interlocking contributory input of multi-layered elements of resources. . . . such as the family, community and society. . . all of which serve to form the 'total education' of the learners – be they children, youth or adult" Occiti (1973). Abagi takes this challenge up within a Eurocentric developmental discourse.

5.6 Teaching African in a Global Context

In a supposedly global age, especially as we rethink African schooling and education in a project to "Teach Africa", the issue of how African schools must adapt to globalization needs addressing. Globalization is nothing new. Globalization today has taken on profound imperialist and colonizing forms. It is generally accepted that the influence of globalization is far-reaching. Scripting human lives, bodies, and communities, globalization has found its way in every facet of the African existence – social, material, physical, spiritual, cultural, political, economic, and psychological. But globalization is and can also be resisted politically and at the discursive levels. Critically teaching Africa demands we respond to globalization in ways that maintain and sustain the African human condition, social existence, and knowledge (Abdi et al. 2006). I believe education has a role to play here.

Even as we herald the achievements and malcontents of the global era, we need to bring a critical lens to read this global epoch.

5.6 Teaching African in a Global Context

According to Abagi (2005) "globalization has brought with it a new global economy." Therein are specific frameworks through which schooling must work. For example, productivity and competitiveness are based on knowledge and information. But whose knowledge and how? There is the Eurocentric framing of time and space. There are no physical or time boundaries or restrictions. Globalization brings with it "the ability to structure the entire planet through telecommunications and computer based informational systems" (Abagi 2005: 309). The faster the school *adapts* to globalization the better the likelihood of its survival in a technological world.

The major challenge for the school [in African contexts] thus lies in developing globally while acting "locally" (Abagi 2005: 309, emphasis added). African schools must "produce dot-com learners and achievers ready and able to cope with and adapt to rapidly changing economic and technological conditions. For example, the school should be able to empower learners to take risks and learn more skills for formal and/or self employment, to make rational decisions to choose, abandon, or change course according to prevailing circumstances. Furthermore a system of school-community partnerships and related apprenticeships might assist learners in identifying their potential while providing on site ICT and other training" (Abagi 2005: 309, emphasis added).

Similarly, there are changing local and global contexts of knowledge production. Martey (2005) sees the conceptualization of education with relations of power and knowledge. To Kom (2005), however, quoting John Beverly, "power is related to representation; [but] which representations have cognitive authority or can secure hegemony and which do not have authority and are not hegemonic?" It is asserted that ".... colonial authority has created the university in Africa by taking careful account not only of the representation it wishes to make of itself through the education dispensed, but also by fixing from the very beginning the image that Africans should have of themselves and of their university studies. And that image is solidly inscribed in subordination" (Kom 2005).

But nowhere does the requirement of critically teaching Africa have a more direct bearing on the global age than in the discussions around difference, identity, citizenship, and belonging. How do we understand the African identity in its complexities and contentions? The struggles for citizenship and nationhood require the evocation of a critical prism informed by local cultural knowings of the African presence in the global community.

Africa is about difference. Such difference is a site of power and social relations. Difference informs experience, everyday practices, and coming to a critical consciousness of life's existence. For development to be pursued in a way respectful of the difference and diversity within communities, knowledge must be contested and appropriately located and engaged. We know that all knowledge is demarcated by class, ability, gender, ethnic, racial, sexual, and cultural locations. The tendency for some groups to impose their knowledge on others is real, and this can and should always be resisted. In an earlier chapter, I discussed Indigenous knowledge and how an anti-colonial framework becomes a discursive means to understand the ways in which "identity" is understood by the people themselves in the aftermath of colonial relations. Colonial refers not simply to North/South, but also to the way in which knowledge can be imposed on others through imperial relations. It is also a discursive approach to interrogate why some knowledge is validated or privileged as opposed to other forms of knowledge. This happens when knowledge along the lines of ability, gender, class, sexuality, or ethnicity is privileged over another form of knowledge (Dei 1999).

We must bring difference in relation to power to the forefront, as we investigate conceptions of development grounded in multiple experiences and locations. Those who have the power to define and design development for Africa speak of the development practice from a particular history. Such history is filled with privilege and complicities. While these may be denied, it is clear to a critical thinker that for development to be meaningful to local peoples, it must speak of everyday local understanding, personal and collective experiences, and social practices. Local peoples have their own understandings of what is happening to them and how they plan to work to improve their lot. They also understand what constitutes development and how they plan to achieve it. Unfortunately, such knowledges are not allowed in the foreground when decisions about human lives are being brokered in the centres of power and authority via the global politics of development. If development is to be achieved and sustained by local peoples, then their own cultural knowledge and actions have to be grounded at the centre of development discourse and practice. Chapter 6 considers how this may be realized.

References

Abagi, O. (2005) The Role of the School in Africa in the Twenty-First Century: Coping with Forces of Changes. In Abdi, A. and Cleghorn, A. (Eds.) *Issues in African Education: Sociological Perspectives* (pp. 297–316). New York: Palgrave Macmillan.
Abdi, A., K. Puplampu, and G. J. S. Dei (Eds.) (2006) *African Education and Globalization: Critical Perspectives*. Lanham, M.D: Lexington Books.
Ake, C. (1982) *Social Science as Imperialism: A Theory of Political Development*. Ibaden: Ibaden University Press.
Black, J. K. (1991) *Development in Theory and Practice: Bridging the Gap*. Boulder, CO: Westview Press.
Chabal, P. (1996) The African Crisis: Context and Interpretation. In Werbner, R. and Ranger, T. (Eds.) *Postcolonial Identities in Africa* (pp. 29–54). London: Zed Books.
Dei, G. J. S. (1999). Interview with Jennifer Kelly. Aurora Online. http://aurora.icaap.org/talks/dei.html .
Escobar, A. (1994) *Encountering Development: The Making and Unmaking of the Third World*. Princeton: Princeton University Press.
Fanon, F. (1967) *The Wretched of the Earth*. New York: Grove Press.
Foucault, M. (1972) *The Archeology of Knowledge*. Sheridan Smith, A. M. (Trans.). New York: Pantheon Books.
Freire, P. (1970) *Pedagogy of the Oppressed*. New York: Continuum.
Kom, A. (2005) Redesigning Africa. *Codesria Bulletin*, (1 and 2), 12–16.
Loomba, A. (1998) *Colonialism/postcolonialism*. New York: Routledge.
Mama, A. (1995) Enslaving the Soul of the Other. In Mama, A. (Ed.) *Beyond the Masks: Race, Gender and Subjectivity* (pp. 17–42). London: Routledge.

References

Martey, J. J. M. (2005) The Challenges of University Governance. *Codesria Bulletin*, (nos 1 and 2), 16–20.
Munck, R. (1999) Deconstructing Development Discourses: Of Impasses, Alternatives and Politics. In Munck, R. and O'Hearn, D. (Eds.) *Critical Development Theory: Contributions to the New Paradigm* (pp. 195–209). London: Zed Books.
Ocitti, J. P. (1973) *African Indigenous Education: As Practiced by The Acholi of Uganda*. Nairobi: East African Literature Bureau.
Rodney, W. (1972) *How Europe Underdeveloped Africa*. Washington, D. C: Howard University Press.
Sardar, Z. (1999) Development and the Location of Eurocentrism. In Munck, R. and O'Hearn, D. (Eds.) *Critical Development Theory: Contributions to the New Paradigm* (pp. 44–61). London: Zed Books.
Smith, L. T. (1999) *Decolonising Methodologies*. London: Zed Books.
Tucker, V. (1999) The Myth of Development: A Critique of Eurocentric Discourse. In Munck, R. and O'Hearn, D. (Eds.) *Critical Development Theory: Contributions to the New Paradigm* (pp. 1–26). London: Zed Books.
wa Thiong'o, N. (1986) *Decolonising the Mind*. New York: Heinemann.

Chapter 6
Reclaiming "Development" Through Indigenity and Indigenous Knowledge

Abstract This chapter focuses on the possibilities of "Indigenous knowledge" from an anti-colonial stance in the pursuit of "African development". The learning objective is to utilize a Ghanaian case study of how local cultural knowledge can be helpful in countering imposed or dominant notions of "development" and "social progress". The chapter considers how Indigenous systems of knowledge are relevant for the promotion of genuine, African-centred development, one that responds to the needs, concerns, and aspirations of peoples of African descent. In fact, we need a critical theoretical lens to imagine and construct viable development options for Africa. By broaching Indigenous and local cultural knowledges and their relevance for African development, local ways of knowing are crucial and relevant to implementing effective social change.

Keywords Development · African development · Indigeneity · Indigenous knowledge · Ghana · Case study · Social progress · African-centred development · Critical theory · Effective social change

6.1 Introduction

From the onset let me assert that there are multiple forms of thinking and explanations of social phenomenon in every society. The dominance of Western systems of thought has been at the expense of devaluing Indigenous ways of knowing. Such devaluation takes the form of ascribing some form of "primitivity" and "backwardness" to Indigenous thought and to argue Indigenous ways of knowing are neither "science or scientific knowledge" nor a valid knowledge system. Reclaiming Indigenous knowledges challenges the racist notion that these knowledges do not exist, are not scientific or logical, or that Indigenous peoples are incapable of scientific thinking and logical deduction. It is interesting that the racist ascription of primitivity to Indigenous knowledge has led to some critical scholars even questioning the validity of Indigenous knowledge. To add insult to injury their critiques and interrogations are often carried out with Western Eurocentric lenses. We cannot ascribe simply theological or metaphysical explanations to Indigenous knowledges. Superstitions abound in all societies, including Western societies. The function of superstitions may differ but they serve to regulate social life and human relationships. Rather than dismiss some forms of knowing, Indigenous knowledge systems offer a more comprehensive and inclusive way of knowing that broach the interfaces of the theological, metaphysical, and the scientific. Indigenous philosophies and traditions offer plausible social explanations and interpretations touching on body–mind–spirit interconnections.

Thus, every system of thought has its own cultural logic that accords a rationality to the knowledge system. All knowledge systems make sense in their cultural contexts. Thus, it is not a question of whether one's thought process is logical and rational and the other is not. It is a matter of the philosophy of knowledge and what a society decides to accord a premium to in the search for social explanations. This explanation is not simply a relativist stance. It is an acknowledgement of the multiple ways of knowing and the principles behind multiple thought systems. Fictive metaphysical and scientific explanations have their own cultural logics and rationality. There is not one form of rationality. Western rationality may be different from Indigenous rationality but each shares ideas and meanings of social phenomena and practice. Indigenous knowledge is the way communities come to understand their world and how we act within such worlds.

In the context of the power and contestations over multiple thought processes, we articulate a connection between Indigenous philosophies and national/social development. A reframing of "African development" would have to focus on the relevance of African Indigenous ways of knowing. Such a focus allows us to understand the multiple ways of knowing, social action, individual and community practice, and their relevance in the causes of social change and human development. What are the local understandings of culture–society–nature interface? What premium is accorded to the spiritual, the mind, and the body in the making of knowledge? How do we understand the Indigenous cultural traditions and cultural resource bases of local peoples and their implications for the pursuit of social development? The predisposing factor of culture helps define in certain contexts the intellectual posture that guides the promotion and pursuit of development (de Graft-Johnston 1977). African-centred development requires the following elements: the understandings of local peoples about the past, present, and the power of human and collective agencies to bring about change; the ability to control their own lives; and desire to set the course of their own development agenda and destiny. These elements are critical to the realization of genuinely African-centred development.

As argued elsewhere (Dei 2000), I use "Indigenous" and "local" interchangeably to denote the complexity, dynamism, and the varied nature of knowledge systems. I also place the discussion in a broader context as a way to rethink development in global contexts. Local peoples ought to be at the forefront in the search for solutions to their problems. Local peoples must interrogate and utilize relevant knowledges from their own histories, Indigenous traditions, and cultures to devise solutions to their current problems. These knowledges cannot be discarded as irrelevant. They

6.1 Introduction

must be interrogated and the sites of empowerment identified in the search for genuine educational options.

There are several and varied components of what constitute Indigenous knowledges: secret societies, local pharmacology, traditions of sustainable forestry, understandings of cosmology, everyday experiential world, traditional farming technologies, and knowledge of soils and climate classifications. What can we learn from these knowledges and how do we protect such knowledges from abuse? These knowledges teach about the ways of life of a people as they make meaning and sense from the relationships of society, culture, and nature. All local communities have long-held traditions and ancestral knowledges passed on from generation to generation. There are knowledges based on everyday experiences of the world. There are knowledges based on intuitions and the cultural logics of communities. These knowledge forms have social purposes. When passed on, there is an expectation of their use to serve human needs and communal well-being. It is important to distinguish "ownership" of knowledge from "custodianship" of such knowledges.

The learner of Indigenous knowledge has a responsibility to use such knowledge for communal benefit. The idea of owning knowledge is not an Indigenous conception of knowledge: Indigenous knowledges is about identity and roots and language is key to understanding Indigenous knowledges. The current discourse of African renaissance can be located in the need to reflect on past experiences and African history and to utilize locally contextualized, cultural knowledges to respond to contemporary pressures. This does not mean a recourse to a mythic or romanticized past, but rather the realization that the past, history, culture and local knowledge have a role to play in fashioning modern solutions. The assertion of local voice is a necessary exercise in resisting domination and colonial imposition. Indigenous knowledge emerges in the immediate context of the livelihoods of local peoples as a product of a sustained process of creative thought and action within communities when local peoples struggle to deal with ever changing set of conditions and problems (see also Agrawal 1995: 5).

Indigenity raises some key questions. Contestations have emerged over what is Indigenous or traditional. The traditional brings the depth of time to social meanings and practices. It is embedded in history and does not stand in opposition to modernity. Tradition reclaims history and the past by resisting an amputation of the past from a people's culture and heritage. The philosophical grounding of an Indigenous knowledge base reaffirms the idea of holism, a connection of the natural and supernatural, an interdependence of culture, society, and nature. Indigenous knowledge is dynamic, undergoing constant modifications as a people negotiate the complex relations with nature, land, culture, and society. Indigenous knowledge is relevant to the extent that it addresses the needs of the community. While this knowledge is localized and context bound, it does not mean it can be boxed in time and space as it transcends boundaries. Speaking about Indigenous knowledges does not, and should not, necessarily commit one to a dichotomy between "Indigenous" and "western knowledge" (Agrawal 1995). Indigenous knowledges do not reveal a conceptual divide with "Western knowledge". Indigenous is not strictly in opposition to "Western". The concept of "Indigenous" is to be thought of in relation to Western knowledge. The concept of "Indigenous" simply alludes to the power relations within which local peoples struggle to define and assert their own representations of history, identity, culture, and place in the face of Western hegemonic ideology/ies. Implicit in the terminology of "indigenous[ness]" is a recognition of some philosophical, conceptual, and methodological differences between Western and non-Western knowledge systems. These differences are not absolutes but matters of degrees.

Difference is seen more in terms of (cultural) logics and epistemologies, including the differences established by context, history, politics, and place. We broach Indigenous knowledge as part of the search for the ways multiple knowledge traditions can be taught in educational settings to offer a comprehensive understanding to society. Knowledge traditions are local and contribute to the development of sustainable futures for local peoples everywhere. Like other knowledge traditions, Indigenous knowledge is culture specific, context bound, political, and subjective. Indigenous knowledge cannot be engaged through a distanced perspective, one in which the claim to know about something or to know about a particular knowledge tradition is based solely or strictly on empirical observation. Indigenous knowledge can be experiential and is practiced in everyday living. It is also revealed in dreams and visions or obtained through intuition (Castellano 2000). This means there is a spirituality to Indigenous knowledge. This does not make such knowledge invalid. In fact, any claims of observable truths, a certainty of knowing, and the comprehensive understanding of all knowledge forms must be tempered with a humility. There is a sacredness of knowing as far as Indigenous knowledges are concerned. Hence, Indigenous knowledge traditions cannot be scrutinized under the gaze of Western positivist thinking.

In the Euro-American contexts, while these knowledge traditions are marginalized in the dominant culture, they have continued to be celebrated by local peoples as embodiments of their identities, histories, and cultures. Christie (2006: 79) enthuses about how such knowledges are "responsive, active and constantly renewed and reconfigured". There is dynamism in the everyday application of Indigenous traditions. Such knowledge achieves its full social effects when shared and collectively engaged. At times the knowledge "is formalized, codified and withdrawn from public access" (Christie 2006:79). Examples include secret societies and knowledge about sacred places. In all cases those who share these knowledges "must account for their right to represent it, [and those] who receive [the knowledge] must reimburse, and be held to account for the use to which it is put" (Christie 2006: 80). This is the responsibility of knowledge and the accountability of knowing. Indigenous knowledge is fundamentally oral and expressive. Through intergenerational transmission of Indigenous traditions the integrity of such knowledge is upheld in communities. The oral transmission of Indigenous philosophies challenges the over-reliance and privileging of printed texts and scripts, what has been termed "scriptocentrism". Indigenous philosophy, as de Certeau (1984: 161) noted, "circulates on the ground within a community of memory and practice" and the privileging of scripts and the written text is a "hallmark of Western imperialism".

In teaching about Africa it is important to articulate the genesis of an ethnoepistemology based on the cultural resource knowledge of local peoples. The

6.1 Introduction

local cultural resource knowledge of African people has been the least studied and analysed for its contributions to the development process. Yet, knowledge of everyday practice sustains livelihoods, responding to both the immediate and long-term pressing needs, concerns, and aspirations of peoples. Such knowledge is "eco-logical" – meaning there are the embedded traditions of sustaining social and natural environmental use that make perfect sense. We can discern such knowledge base from the following sources: oral traditions; the significance of cultural artifacts; the cultural expressions conveyed in local proverbs, folklore, parables, stories, and mythologies; the examination and study of local fauna and flora; the sustainable use of biological diversity knowledge; the rituals of secret societies, cultural festivals, and the performing arts; local craftsmanship; and the functioning of local customary laws. Our research needs to consider these aspects: the cultural preservation of such knowledge forms, their sources, and everyday uses and applications; how such knowledges have been historically constructed; the producers of specific cultural and community artifacts; and the purposes and significance of these cultural resources. All of these aspects point to rich sources of ethno-epistemology or Indigenous philosophy.

The cultural protocols behind the engagement of these knowledge forms inherently speak of the validity of Indigenous science. The protocols also recognize the need to link Indigenous knowledge, innovations, and practices to formal (school) science knowledge, conservation practices, and the broad questions of sustainable development. These knowledge forms can be engaged in schools, colleges, and universities to help learners understand the ways of knowing of local peoples, the socio-political contexts of the production of ethno-philosophies, and the complexities of local knowledges. The sovereignty, ownership, control, and protection of such Indigenous knowledge forms and their cultural manifestations must be recognized and respected. Indigenous peoples are custodians of their knowledges. The sharing of such knowledges must adhere to this basic understanding or fundamental affirmation. Younging (2007) cautions that "the categorization of Indigenous knowledge and some information such as medicinal plants, sacred sites or particular spiritual practices, customs and traditions...cannot be for monetary benefits" (31). The social practices, rituals, and festivals point to knowledge concerning the interface of nature, culture, and society. We need educational frameworks that can help revitalize Indigenous knowledges; in so doing, we help strengthen ties between Elders and youth.

I have identified some basic Indigenous principles that guide African systems of thought (Dei 1996). I reiterate these principles as common underlying themes of African knowledge to emphasize the power of local Indigenousness in the search for genuine development options for African peoples. I note that, in fact, African peoples do not have a monopoly over such knowledges. These knowledges can be shared and experienced by other Indigenous communities. I merely reiterate these as significant to the functioning of African communities. The principles constitute the everyday sense-making of integrating culture, history, and questions of identity of African peoples. I refer specifically to the epistemic saliency of cultural traditions, values, belief systems, and world views of society that are imparted to the younger generation by community Elders. Such knowledge constitutes an

Indigenous informed epistemology. This is a world view that shapes the community's relationships with its environments. It is the product of the direct experience of nature and its relationship with the social world. It is knowledge that is essential for the survival of society. It is knowledge that is "Indigenous" in the sense of resulting from long-term residence in a place. In most Indigenous African communities certain social values were singled out for emphasis. For example, among the major themes emphasized in Indigenous African ways of knowing are the ideas of community membership, social responsibility, cohesiveness, and the commonality of all peoples. Such ideas and knowledge are expressed in local traditions, cultural beliefs, traditional songs, fables, proverbs, legends, and mythologies.

Knowledge–Experience Nexus: All knowledge is accumulated knowledge, based on observing and experiencing the social and natural worlds. This principle recognizes the link between knowledge and experience. It also takes the position that there is no sole authority on knowledge. The presence of cultural and political repositories of traditional knowledge in communities does not necessarily imply individual or group exclusive ownership of, exclusive use of, or control over knowledge production and dissemination.

Social Learning: We are all learners of the social and natural world. Social learning has to be personalized in order to develop the intuitive and analytical aspects of the human mind. In other words, every way of knowing is subjective and based in part on experiential knowledge. Such personal subjective identification with the learning processes makes it possible for the individual to be invested spiritually and emotionally in the cause of social change. It is particularly emphasized that the acquisition of knowledge is a process of interactions between the body, mind, and the human spirit. The action of thought is a causal factor in social action.

Interactive Processes: All knowledge is socially and collectively created through the interactive processes between individuals, groups, and the natural worlds. This principle acknowledges the dynamism of knowledge and its continual process through daily interactions. The principle does not attribute knowledge acquisition simply to individual acumen, talent, or to the limits of one's own senses. Knowledge comes from individual, family, communal, and human–nature interactions. The principle involves the collective activities of the social group and the natural and spiritual forces of the world. For instance, this process is reflected in the power of the ancestors and gods.

Human-Natural Connections: Humans are part of the natural world. We do not stand apart and neither are we above the natural world. This principle affirms that our basic humanness is a value system which speaks to the importance of relating to, rather than dominating, nature and the environment. This humanness stresses points of conciliation, interdependence, and connections. It challenges a presentation of the universe as a world to be studied and dominated.

Holism: To understand one's social reality is to have a holistic view of society. It is conceded that the social, political, material, religious, spiritual structures of society are connected to each other. For example, we cannot separate politics from economics, culture, religion, cosmology, family, and kinship.

6.1 Introduction

Human Agency: History and social change are processes which do not completely lie outside the purview and power of human agency. Humans have agency and power to control the course of their destiny to some point. While the act of change itself is sacred, humans can predict and cause social change with the blessing of the powers of the natural world. Ancestral spirits are examples.

Metaphysics: Both our social and natural worlds are full of uncertainties. The metaphysical world cannot be explained away through cause and effect relationships. In other words, there is no certainty in any knowledge. Every way of knowing is clouded by some uncertainty about the social and natural worlds. Humans do not need to strive and explain away everything about their world. Mythologies constitute a powerful base of knowledge that cannot be dismissed as frivolous, superstitious, illogical, and "unscientific".

Preservation: Humans do not possess the Earth. We have a responsibility to preserve what is accorded to us by our preceding generation. We are accountable to a higher order for our actions, a higher order beyond the capacity of the human senses to comprehend. As living beings we have borrowed the Earth from our ancestors. The living would incur the wrath of the ancestors if they destroyed nature in the process of satisfying societal and individual material needs.

Individual–Community Nexus: Both concepts of "individual" and "community" are important. They are linked to and need each other. However, the concept of the individual only makes sense in relation to the community of which he or she is part. The collective spirit is stronger than the individual mind. The uniqueness of the individual is recognized in terms of her or his personality, spiritual essence, talents, and "destiny". However, it is argued that such individuality must be defined and placed in the wider social and political contexts. Similarly, the community is a "community of differences" whose uniqueness and sameness is simultaneously defined by its constituted members. The principle makes a distinction between a "co-operative individual", one who is nurtured and bolstered by a community of other, and a "competitive individual", one who shuns a collectivity and is protective of his or her gains, is ruled by his individualistic instincts.

Rights and Responsibilities: Rights are only meaningful in the contexts of matching responsibilities. It is the meeting of these responsibilities that strengthens the rights accorded to individuals, groups, and communities. The rights of membership in social contexts come with an expectation of social conduct that strengthens the community. The existence of the community is a defence mechanism to protect the rights of the individual.

Interconnections: Every life form exists in paired relationships that are interconnected (Holmes 1996). Thus, there are no such fine distinctions in life – young/old, individual/communal, mind/body, personal/political, and the social/natural. To deal with these facts of life, it is contended that humans need a non-dualistic mode of thought that balances all social and natural relationships. In other words, Indigenous ways of knowing are not based on fragmented categories. This principle also recognizes that humans live in a continuous rather than a fixed, linear time frame.

Living Knowledge: Knowledge and survival go hand in hand. In other words, knowledge is for survival, and all knowledge must compel action. Knowledge is meaningful when lived and practised. Knowledge cannot be simply an abstract thought. Every knowledge is a "living document". Knowledge must be actualized in everyday practice. Consequently, we cannot separate theory from practice. The key to human survival is the ability of society to pass knowledge down through generations by cultural transmission.

These Indigenous African philosophical principles are conveyed in societal modes of thought, including songs, dances, proverbs, stories, fables, tales, popular culture, and the performing arts, to regulate and guide individual and collective human action, thought, and behaviour. There are important lessons for teaching and learning about Africa and the culture, history, and traditions of peoples of African descent.

6.2 Indigenous Knowledge, Schooling, Education and African Development: Connecting the Dots

What is the educative, instructional, and pedagogic relevance of the foregoing principles of Indigenous African knowledge systems? How do these knowledges connect to the search for genuine development options for Africa and African peoples? What are the responsibilities of schools in such endeavours? In this discussion, I use "development" in the wider sense of general well-being and collective welfare. In the remainder of this chapter, I look at two sites for teaching about African Indigenous knowledges to promote both schooling and social development. First, let us consider the relevance of Indigenous knowings emerging from African proverbs, folktales, and stories in enhancing youth education through the promotion of social values for strong moral character teaching. Second, let us think about the knowledges and teachings of traditional medicine and healing, specifically local pharmacology, and their roles in enhancing community health and science education.

6.3 African Proverbs, Folktales and Stories: Pedagogic and Instructional Relevance in the Promotion of Moral and Character Education

The philosophical principles of African Indigenous knowledge systems discussed so far are about social conduct and values of communities. Schools, families, and communities need to enter into meaningful partnerships to impact community morals and values education for youth. In conventional schooling, moral education was part of civic education where youth were taught the values and morals of society. Learners were also trained in civic responsibilities and requirements of nationhood and citizenship. Traditional schooling and education were about creating a society or community of love. These ideas need to be revisited in contemporary schooling. This is critical since the link between education and development cannot simply be assumed. It must be theorized and operationalized in ways that make it possible to reproduce knowledge for genuine African development.

There are huge responsibilities for African education today. Education should be about development of the body, mind, and soul. Education must make the learner whole and recognize her or his responsibility to the community they are part of. For educators, school administrators, and policy workers, we must direct our gaze beyond the conventional focus on credits, certification, and accreditation to the examination of questions about content and purpose of education, who is receiving education, what is being taught in schools, and how we get all students to learn. These priorities necessitate shifting the focus away from performance indicators to examining how students feel about themselves and their schooling. Educators can encourage and motivate students to learn by grounding knowledge in the everyday experiences of the learner. It is also relevant that educators create spaces in schools for students to develop a sense of ownership in the creation and production of knowledge. In other words, what can our students teach us in schools?

In the African contexts, as in North America, there is a growing body of work dealing with the broad theme of "Indigenous knowledges". We also have a number of texts that have documented African proverbs and their cultural meanings and interpretations (Kudadjie 1996; Yankah 1989, 1995; Opoku 1997, 1975; Ogede 1993; Kalu 1991; Pachocinshi 1996; Abubakre and Reichmuth 1997). Much of the focus has been on proverbs. Folklore, fables, parables, tales, and mythologies have received scant attention. Arguably, the issue of local cultural resource knowledge, as contained in proverbs, parables, fables, mythologies, and folklore, offers specific pedagogic, instructional, and communicative enhancements to learning outcomes for youth in contemporary school settings. These contributions have not received adequate critical exploration (Boateng 1990; Bascom 1965). Yet these local cultural knowings are relevant for the lessons they offer in promoting the goals of collective responsibility, community building, mutual interdependence, and meeting rights and responsibilities of citizenship. These knowledges also affirm the importance of multiple knowings in schooling and education. The diversity in North American schools makes this inquiry relevant given our contingent and complex histories, cultures, and experiences demarcated by race, gender, class, sexual, linguistic, and religious differences.

Many communities utilize proverbs, parables, folktales, and mythologies to convey meanings of society, nature, and cultural interactions (Abrahams 1967, 1968a, b, 1972; Dorson 1972; Taylor 1934; Wolfgang and Dundas 1981). We know that Aboriginal traditions focus more on storytelling than proverbs and fables. In Aboriginal epistemology we see how story telling conveys powerful meanings similar to those encoded in proverbs, parables, fables, and tales in other Indigenous contexts (Firth 1926). Within the stories a critical learner can get a powerful sense of the pedagogic, instructional, and communicative relevance of such cultural knowings. For example, Johnson (1993, 2003) shows Ojibway mythology as having rich, complex, and dense meaning and mystery. His works provide readers with a succinct understanding of Ojibway people's lives, legends, and beliefs. Like stories and mythologies, proverbs, when told, often evoke an act of self-reflection from the learner/listener. As powerful knowledge forms, proverbs, folktales, and stories offer a deeper level of understanding and appreciation of the community's place in the larger social/physical/cultural realm of life. Selected writings (Chamberlain 2003; Eastman and Nerburn 1993; Hill and Norbert 1999; and Stiffarm 1998) point out a current globalized and transnational world; it is a world wherein we continually encounter competing claims to land, resources, power, and such knowledge sources as proverbs, tales, folktales, and mythologies. These sources can be helpful to all learners in appreciating the common thread of human existence.

Character and moral development are equally questions of spiritual development of the learner. Therefore, education must be about an affirmation of students' spiritualities and identities. Within traditional African cultures, moral and values education is conveyed through the lessons of proverbs, songs, fables, tales, and stories that point to the need to reorient the learner to the responsibilities of community membership. Morals, values, and character education is about education of a community. Moral education, as a form of spiritual education, would begin in the home with the foundations of a strong character development for the learner. The responsibilities of families, homes, and caregivers extended beyond the narrow confines of the immediate home environment to the wider community. Educating the learners is a shared responsibility between the home, families, communities, and schools.

Whether in the homes, families, or schools, the teachings of social responsibility, citizenship, respect, discipline, and sense of purpose are considered the bedrock of moral and values education. In schools, teachers' success in moral and character development of young learners partly depends on the moral conduct of the educators themselves as they interact with their students. Teaching discipline and respect entails teaching about spiritual, moral, and cultural values of the community. Discipline cannot simply be enforced. It must be taught. Indiscipline can be due to youth alienation from cultures and their schools. It entails a search for a more broad definition of violence – the ways educators pursue or promote the learning process via tone, content, dress, and non-verbal communication. These sites can and do reveal sources and traces of violence in education. The varying nature and degree of violence also entails that the enforcement of discipline must be context-specific. One size cannot fit all. The environment under which discipline is enforced is equally important. Discipline and punishment must address the question of relevancy. Punishment must fit the crime. It must be reformative, not punitive. It must be educational, rather than turning youth into irresponsible citizens. Expulsion from school should be the last resort and reserved for very serious forms of violent crimes.

It is also acknowledged that what constitutes "moral values" can be contested by different communities. Attempts at moral and values education as part of character development of youth must engage the question of difference and its contestations. Furthermore, values education is more than teaching moral values. It is about developing positive attitudes among youth, motivating youth to learn to acquire skills that will make them contribute to society building. Moral education is respect for Elders, authority, and community. Moral education is helping youth develop confidence in their learning. Moral and character development is grooming youth to be responsible citizens and adults.

Teaching Africa calls for a critical search for avenues, spaces, and mediums for effective education. What can African and North American education gain by working with the multiple sources of knowledge contained in Indigenous knowledge traditions, including local proverbs, folktales, fables, mythologies, and story telling? This question is significant in the current push to make education more relevant to students' needs, aspirations, and experiences, and to connect questions of culture, history, politics, identity, and local knowledge in the delivering of education to diverse youth. Moral and values education can also be pursued for the youth through popular culture, especially art, music, songs, drama, and theatre. Indigenous proverbs, fables, parables, tales, and mythologies contain significant teachings and pedagogical lessons for educating about Africa. Through the examination of proverbs, fables, parables, tales, and mythologies we can articulate an Indigenous philosophy for learning and teaching relevant to education of youth in African and North American contexts. Our schools, like schools in Africa and elsewhere, continue to search for more effective ways of delivering education to a diverse group of learners. Local cultural resource knowledge, when used critically, can be an important source of information and a tool for educational delivery for students. Unfortunately, as repeatedly noted, the cultural knowings of local communities have been the least emphasized in the search for genuine educational options for our youth. In African contexts, the literary works of Chinua Achebe (1966), Ayi Kwei Armah (1969), and Ngugi wa Thiong'o (1965, 1986) point to how local African proverbs, parables, fables, myths, mythologies, and folklore contain words of wisdom, instruction, and knowledge about society. These cultural knowings have a long history of connecting cultures, traditions, and histories of diverse groups of people while offering understandings of the complex interactions of society, nature, and culture. These knowledges teach about individual and communal responsibility, sense of direction, and purpose. They also help educate about the requirements of community belonging, citizenship, and the importance of affirming myriad identities.

Hence, educators need to explore and understand the particular teachings central to the African cultural resource knowledge base through local proverbs, parables, fables, myths, and folktales. We also need to examine the specific instructional, pedagogic, and communicative values and challenges offered in these teachings. It is significant that educators themselves understand the ways local cultural resource knowledge can be engaged to enhance learning for a diverse group of students. Educators must also examine the extent to which local cultural knowledges address questions of diversity and difference, including race/ethnicity, gender, class, sexuality, [dis]ability, language, and cultural and religious differences, and the implications for promoting inclusive education in pluralistic contexts.

6.4 Traditional Medicine

There are some key issues and challenges in the study of traditional medicine and plant pharmacology as Indigenous forms of knowing. Traditional medicine and Indigenous herbalists are assumed to be assisting with community health care needs and national development. However, the linkage needs to be theorized and operationalized, the sociological and educational dimensions fleshed out for the understanding of society–nature–culture nexus. By identifying some key questions, the discussion hopes to broach the challenges and possibilities of educational research in providing relevant knowledge for the theorization of Indigenity as a valid way of knowing in the academy.

Among the key research questions for exploration are as follows: What are the philosophical and epistemological bases of traditional medicine and local plant pharmacology in Indigenous knowledge systems? How can such knowledge be studied? How do we deal with issues of custodianship of these knowledges? How can these knowledges be communicated across communities? How to ensure authenticity and avoid misappropriation? What are the ethnic, gender, age, class, and intergenerational dimensions of these knowledge forms? How do we introduce these knowledges into the school science curriculum? It is widely recognized in Africa that there is the need for the integration of traditional medicinal knowledge into school science and social studies curriculum. Knowledge about plant medicine could be helpful in developing appropriate instructional and pedagogic approaches to the teaching of Indigenous science. An understanding of the traditional ways of knowledge transfer in communities, including inter-generational communication, gendered dimensions of traditional knowledge, and working with traditional cultural custodians, herbalists, and medical practitioners, point to the sociocultural and political contexts of Indigenous science education.

There is growing public and academic interest in complementary medicines. The knowledge systems of traditional medicine and herbal medicine are not so distinct from each other. The differences are increasingly becoming blurred in our communities today. In fact, traditional medicine is inclusive of herbal medicine. They both constitute Indigenous forms of knowledge dealing specifically with the health and social well-being of a community. Many herbalists and traditional medical practitioners are embracing the social, cultural, natural, spiritual, and physical realms of everyday existence. They are depending on the material and non-material, the physical and metaphysical, and the interface of such meanings in their communities. What does the distinction and the coordination of such knowledge systems, especially traditional medicine and plant medicine, mean for teaching science and technology?

An important methodological issue to be noted is the documentation of these knowledge systems for wider educative purposes in communities, not just at health clinics. There is also the challenge of archiving information for future reference and education. This will entail knowing who and what are the appropriate sources in the acquisition of these knowledges. This in itself it helpful to deal with the question of ownership of knowledge, including intellectual property rights. Recognizing the necessity of subterfuge and discretion for the survival of this knowledge, in some communities the secrecy and rituals surrounding traditional medicine constitute a gate-keeping process for survival.

6.5 Conclusion

Local subjects are embedded in an awareness of the self and one's place within a collective. Knowing the self, community, and culture is important in order to appreciate the challenges and how we respond. Since Indigenity and issues of identity are powerfully linked, we cannot dismiss the power of Indigenous and local cultural knowings. Local knowings contained in proverbs and parables are significant for expressing the intellectual agency of communities. Local cultural resource knowledge, one that allows for a critical reflection on past experiences and histories to respond to everyday problems, is very relevant. Claiming such knowledge does not mean recourse to a mythic or romanticized past. It is a realization that the past, a people's history, and local cultural resource base have roles to play in the search for answers to daily concerns and problems.

As educators, we must question the knowledge we teach and why we teach these knowings. In the ongoing search for critical ways to rethink schooling and education through knowledge production, there must be effective and meaningful classroom pedagogy and instruction, borrowed from and informed by varied communities. In documenting local proverbs, parables, fables, mythologies, and folklore, the research interest lies in the pedagogic, instructional, and communicative significance for African and Canadian students. By working with local educators and cultural resource experts, the goal is to bring multiple knowings to bear on the education of students in pluralistic contexts.

There is educational relevance in the documentation of proverbs, fables, folktales, and myths. They offer insights into Indigenous philosophies, ideas, and concepts that cannot be lost to future generations. Such Indigenous cultural resource knowledges demonstrate ways societies deal with the tensions, contradictions, and challenges of tradition and modernity. Pedagogically, instructionally, and communicatively, these Indigenous cultural knowings inform notions of "schooling as community" and learners' rights and responsibilities to self and others. These cultural knowings educate us about learning as a cooperative and collaborative undertaking. Despite the many successes, each day we are confronted with youth who are disaffected in society, disengaged in schools, and disturbingly see violence as a solution to problems. How can these cultural knowings be evoked in schooling and education of the youth to inculcate in all learners a sense of hope, agency, resistance, responsibility, personal discipline, and respect? How do these Indigenous cultural knowings teach about citizenship, rights, social responsibility, mutual interdependence, and societal obligations? These cultural knowings speak about ways to resolve daily human problems and social conflicts through power sharing. They help inform about human nature and the power of society/nature/culture interactions. They provide cultural information filled with wit and wisdom to learners. They teach about ways we use knowledge to compel social action. I see such knowledge as critical for all societies, and particularly for pluralistic communities. Contemporary education must respond to the challenge of global citizenship by working with the multiple knowledges of diverse communities.

The study of proverbs offers educative opportunities for us to rethink schooling and education. As embodiments of local cultural morals and norms, proverbs offer the learner an opportunity and the space to flesh out the complexities and contradictions of everyday life. Proverbs point to the ways through which the words and advice of Elders offer poignant cues to problem solving. Proverbs are not only about a higher level of conceptual thinking. They are the theoretical pillars around which everyday communication can assume meaning in society and offer lessons for youth as they navigate the complexities and nuances of the world. The intellectual, political, and spiritual resistance of dominant knowledge cannot materialize if educators fail to rethink the possibilities of education. Knowledge is not just about power but also about the organization of social thought. Knowledge is meaningful when it offers possibilities for a people to construct meaning and understanding in the everyday politics of information use and dissemination.

The challenges facing the study of fables, folktales, and mythologies for their instructional and pedagogic value include the issues of documentation and how such documentation should be carried out. We know in most African and Indigenous communities Elders are cultural custodians of language and embrace the generational transmission of this knowledge

Who can teach proverbs and how? The understanding of the local language is a starting point for a study of proverbs. In teaching African proverbs in North American schools, an educator must address the problem of wrestling such knowledge from its appropriate contexts. Proverbs are subject to multiple and varied interpretations. Interpretations can be cultural and context specific. Drawing upon this foundation, Chapter 7 provides practical strategies for the engagement of African-centred teaching and learning.

References

Abrahams, R. (1967) On Proverb Collecting and Proverb Collection. *Proverbium*, 8, 181–184.
Abrahams, R. (1968a) A Rhetoric of Everyday Life: Traditional Conversational Genres. *Southern Folklore Quarterly*, 32, 44–59.
Abrahams, R. (1968b) Introductory Remarks in a Rhetorical Theory of Folklore. *Journal of American Folklore*, 81, 143–158.
Abrahams, R. (1972) Proverbs and Proverbial Expression. In Dorson, R. (Ed.) *Folklore and Folklife* (pp. 117–127). Chicago: Chicago University Press.
Abubakre, R. D. and Reichmuth, S. (1997) Arabic Writing Between Global and Local Culture: Scholars and Poets in Yorubaland. *Research in African Literatures*, 28(3), 183–209.
Achebe, C. (1996) *Things Fall Apart*. Oxford; Portsmouth, NH: Heinemann Educational.
Agrawal, A. (1995) Dismantling the Divide Between Indigenous and Scientific Knowledge. *Development and Change*, 26, 413–439.
Armah, A. K. (1969) *The Beautiful Ones Are Not Yet Born*. New York: Collier Books.

References

Bascom, W. (1965) The Forms of Folklore: Prose Narratives. *Journal of American Folklore*, 78(307), 3–20.

Battiste, M. A. and Henderson, J. Y. (Eds) (2000) *Protecting Indigenous Knowledge and Heritage: A Global Challenge*. Saskatoon: Purich.

Boateng, F. (1990) African Traditional Education: A Tool for Intergenerational Communication. In Asante, M. K. and Asante, K. W. (Eds.) *African Culture: The Rhythms of Unity* (pp. 109–122). Trenton: African World Press.

Castellano, M. B. (2000) Updating Aboriginal Traditions of Knowledge. In Dei, G. J. S., Hall Budd L, and D. Goldin Rosenberg, B. (Eds.) *Indigenous Knowledges in Global Contexts: MulTiple Readings of Our World* (pp. 21–36). Toronto: University of Toronto Press.

Chamberlain, T. (2003) *If This is Your Land, Where Are Yoru Stories?: Finding Common Ground*. Toronto: Alfred A. Knopf Canada.

Christie, M. (2006) Transdisciplinary Research and Aboriginal Knowledge. *The Australian Journal of Indigenous Education*, 35, 78–89.

De Certeau, M. (1984) *The Practice of Everyday Life*. Berkeley, CA: University of California Press.

De Graft-Johnson, K. E. (1977). "Fictive Thinking and Social Development". Unpublished paper, Department of Sociology, University of Ghana, Legon.

Dei, G. J. S. (1996) *Anti-Racism Education: Theory and Practice*. Halifax, Nova Scotia: Fernwood Publishing.

Dei, G. J. S. (2000) Rethinking the Role of Indigenous Knowledges in the Academy. *International Journal of Inclusive Education*, 4(2), 111–132.

Dorson, R. (Ed.) (1972) *Folklore and Folklife*. Chicago: University of Chicago Press.

Eastman, C. A. and Nerburn, K. (Eds.) (1993) *The Soul of an Indian and Other Writings from Ohiyesa (The Classic Wisdom Collection)*. New York: New World Library.

Firth, R. (1926) Proverbs in the Native Life with Particular Reference to Those of the Maori. *Folklore*, 32.

Hill Jr., Norbert S. (Ed.) (1999) *Words of Power: Voices from Indian America*. New York: Fulcrum Publishing.

Holmes, L. (1996) *Elders' Knowledge and the ancestry of experience in Hawaii*. (Unpublished Ph.D thesis at the University of Toronto/OISE, Department of Sociology and Equity Studies).

Johnson, B. (1993) *Ojibway Tales*. Nebraska: University of Nebraska Press.

Johnson, B. (2003) *Ojibway Heritage*. Toronto: McClelland and Stewart.

Kalu, O. U. (1991) Gender Ideology in Igbo Religion: The Changing Religious Role of Women in Igboland. *Africa/Istituto Italo-Africano,*, 46(2), 184–202.

Kudadjie, J. N. (1996). *Ga and Dangme Proverbs: For Preaching and Teaching*. Accra: Asempa Publishers. Retrieved on March 29, 2009. http://www.crvp.org/book/Series02/II-5/chapter_iii.htm

Ogede, O. S. (1993) The Role of the Igede Poet Micah Ichegbeh's "Adiyah" Songs in the Political and Moral Education of his Local Audiences. *African Languages and Cultures*, 6(1), 49–68.

Opoku, K. A. (1975) *Speak to the Winds: Proverbs from Africa*. New York: Northrop: Lee & Shepard Co.

Opoku, K. A. (1997) *Hearing and Keeping: Akan Proverbs*. Accra: Asempa Publishers.

Pachocinshi, R. (1996). *Proverbs of Africa: Human Nature in the Nigerian Oral Tradition: An Exposition and Analysis of 2,600 Proverbs from 64 Peoples'*. Continuum International Publishing. Online: http://www.paragonhouse.com/catalog/product_info.php?cPath=23_46&products_id=155http://www.paragonhouse.com/catalog/product_info.php?cPath=23_46&products_id=155

Stiffarm, L. A. (Ed.) (1998) *As We See ... Aboriginal Pedagogy*. Saskatoon: University Extension Press. Saskatoon: University of Saskatchewan.

Taylor, A. (1934) Problems in the Study of Proverbs. *Journal of American Folklore*, 47, 1–21.

Wolfgang, M. and Dundas, A. (1981) *The Wisdom of Many: Essays on the Proverb*. New York: Garland Publishing.

wa Thiong'o, N. (1965) *The River Between*. London: Heinemann.
wa Thiong'o, N. (1986) *Decolonizing the Mind: The Politics of Language in African Literature*. London: James Currey.
Yankah, K. (1989) *The Proverb in the Content of Akan Rhetoric: A Theory Proverb Praxis*. Bern, Frankfurt au Main: Peter Lang.
Yankah, K. (1995) *Speaking for the Chief: Okyeame and the Politics of Akan Oratory*. Bloomington & Indianapolis: Indiana University Press.
Younging, G. (2007). Traditional Knowledge in the International Framework. Paper presented at the Annual conference on: Indigenous Knowledge and Indigenous Science. Australia Indigenous Studies Association, Sydney, Australia, July 11–14, 2007.

Chapter 7
Indigenous Knowledge! Any One? Pedagogical Possibilities for Anti-colonial Education

Abstract Extending the discussion beyond the theoretical justification for African-centred education, this chapter demonstrates how identity and knowledge production are concrete tools for learning. The lived experiences of Indigeneity – the particularities of location and experiences – inform how theory guides the teaching and learning processes.

Keywords Pedagogy · Anti-colonialism · Anti-colonial education · African-centred education · Identity production · Knowledge production · Learning tools · Indigeneity · Locality · Teaching and learning processes

7.1 Introduction

The learning objective of this chapter is to move Indigenous knowledge as part of the 'contest of the marginals' in terms of the way oppositional and minority discourses and bodies are positioned in the academy to compete among themselves to serve the interests of the dominant. This chapter calls for a recognition and acknowledgement of Indigenous knowledge as legitimate knowledge in its own right and not in competition with other sources or forms of knowledge. Power and ambition work in compelling ways to situate bodies differently in the Western academy. It is part of playing the game on the basis of rules determined by the dominant. For example, I argue that we cannot evaluate the philosophical grounding and social worth of Indigenous philosophies using Eurocentric lenses. In reframing ideas of a paper initially presented as a keynote address at a conference on 'Indigenous Knowledge' in Sydney, Australia (Dei 2008), I have embarked upon a project that offers an opportunity for me to continue on the decolonial/anti-colonial intellectual journey in ways informed by anti-colonial and Indigenous theorists. In this journey, I want to highlight my own African agency and interrogate Indigenous knowledge as part of the contemporary critical intellectual traditions articulating emancipator discourses for colonized subjects. The recognition of Indigenous knowledge as legitimate in its own right requires that we rethink the spaces that are currently in place for nurturing and sustaining a healthy multiplicity of knowledges. I would argue that we not only have to decolonize existing spaces but also create new ones. We cannot simply ask hegemonic spaces to make room for other knowledges to co-exist. The politics and activism of de-centring spaces and knowledges require that we rethink new ways of creating knowledge systems so as to deal with power inequities. The liberal relativist stance and, to some extent, the post-modernism, creating spaces for all voices, ideas, and standpoints to be heard, can only be seductive and end of affirming the dominance of particular forms of knowledge. Not all knowledges have the same power and influence in our academics. This chapter attempts to create spaces of resistance for these ideas to emerge.

I come to this discussion with humility from an interested and politicized position. Pohlhaus (2002) long ago argued that "objective knowledge" is not a disinterested perspective. Instead, it "is achieved by struggling to understand one's experience through a critical stance on the social order within which knowledge is produced". (285, cited in Nakata 2007).

My vested interests in and political engagement with inclusive, equitable education leads me to begin this chapter by raising issues pertaining to our collective responsibility to nurture the next generation of Indigenous scholars. How do we Indigenize our "Other" of Indigenous knowledges, the University? How do we help our next generation of Indigenous scholars thrive and get their work done in an environment that is an improvement on the one we experienced? This chapter then moves to highlight aspects of current theorizing of Indigenity: the search for epistemological equity through a reclamation of identity, knowledge, and politics of embodiment. In searching for epistemological equity my interest is not in a claim of "epistemic relativism" but in what I call "epistemic saliency". In other words, how does the knowledge about our own existence, realities, and identities help produce a form of knowing legitimate in its own right and able to contest other ways of knowing? In particular, I identify some principles essential to the development of a critical Indigenous discursive framework. The discussion concludes with what I see as some of the pedagogical possibilities of anti-colonial education using the Indigenous framework.

Claiming Indigenous knowledge in the Western academy is an anti-colonial struggle for independence from exploitative relations of schooling and knowledge production. Anti-colonial pedagogy is resisting the trappings of colonial and imperial education. It implies a resistance to amputation and offers an intellectual challenge to those who would subjugate Indigenous peoples' knowings and experiences. Indigenous knowledge is about cultural rootedness and groundedness in place and history. Anti-colonial education theorizes the "Indigenous" beyond its current boundaries and spatialization, seeking to create a discursive synthesis of different knowledges, important aspects of Indigenous philosophies and ontologies.

Let me apologize from the onset for anything I am going to say that might offend someone. In writing this text, I had to take on two main voices: the voice of the "creator/producer" of ideas and the voice informed by the spiritual Elder. Seeking a union of academic and authentic voices, it has been a challenge to create the transition between and around these voices for them to work together in an essay/speech.

I have always insisted on awareness. If we are humble in our claims to know, we will usually take leave of any place knowing more! In addition to constantly seeking to speak truth to power, we must also insist that power speaks truth to us. This means we must insist on meeting the desires of social responsibility and accountability from those in positions of power and influence; we must acknowledge the injustices that afflict wide segments of our community.

I am always mindful of evoking the "US" as it implies a "THEM". But I use "US" to denote an "epistemic community" that shares a political and academic project that heralds the power of Indigeneity and subverts the tendency for certain knowledges to masquerade as universal knowledge, particularly in the academy.

Recently, a colleague asked if I would choose "identity" over "dignity". My response: "Why this choice in the first place?" It is a false binary choice. How can we speak of "dignity" in the absence of "identity"? When dignity is uncoupled from identity, our existence is hollow, founded only on the emptiness of material gratification.

7.2 Revealing Biases Within

In March 2007, I read a column in Canada's national newspaper about the Muslim scholar, Ayaan Hirsi, who now lives in the United States. She had originally emigrated from Somalia to Holland. An ardent critic of Islam, a position much loved in some Western circles, Ayaan has this to say: "Colonization and slavery have created a sentiment of culpability in the West that leads people to adulate foreign traditions...This is a lazy even racist attitude." She then goes further to argue that the ideals of Enlightenment belong to the entire human race, not just the West. I would agree with this latter point, but she adds that "Western liberal culture is superior to Islamic tribal group culture...If you want to feel guilty, feel guilty that you didn't bring John Stuart Mill and left us only with the Koran" (Wente 2007: A25). This is intellectually lazy if not outright dishonest. For a minority scholar to privilege Western systems of thought by decrying the value of other cultures shows that anti-colonial politics have a long way to go.

Furthermore, the West is complicit in colonialism, colonization, and enslavement. It is not simply "culpable". But the struggle is not really a struggle to decolonize. Rather, as Graham Smith "Personal Communication. [April 2]. University British Columbia, Vancouver, BC, 2007" notes, it is a challenge to Indigenize our thought processes and institutions. As Indigenous scholars and pursuers of Indigenous knowledge and scholarship, we can neither afford a misreading nor an amputation of history. We cannot contribute to the process of self-destruction of our knowledges by failing to bring a critical eye to the interrogation of questions of Indigeneity. Embedded in Indigenous knowledges is the idea of universality of shared values. This could be our contribution to the ways we rethink the crisis of knowledge and its production in our institutions and communities.

Indigeneity is distinct, albeit related, to the question of Aboriginality. Indigenous philosophies and Aboriginal epistemologies share many ideas in common. While

Aboriginality makes specific cultural claims, Indigeneity brings an expanded internationalized dimension to debates about Indigenousness. Nonetheless, I admit that Indigenous philosophies and Aboriginal epistemologies share many ideas in common.

In this chapter, I operate from an anti-colonial Indigenous prism or discursive stance. My argument is that the dominance of Eurocentricity, as it operates in the Western academy, is part of the colonial encounter. The radical critiques of anti-colonial thinkers are firmly rooted in material, political, and spiritual analyses of our daily existence. But unlike Marxist/Neo-Marxist traditions, an anti-colonial Indigenous epistemology sees the 'spiritual', not the material, at the base rather than at the substructure. Any anti-colonial theorizing of Indigeneity and Aboriginality must look at epistemological engagements with power at the levels of material, systemic, symbolic, and spiritual. Such a discursive position implicates an understanding of the salient aspects of Eurocentricity, particularly as it pertains to questions of knowledge production and Indigenous scholarship.

In 1903, W. E. B. Du Bois proclaimed that the problem of the twentieth century was the colour line. I would restate that for the twenty-first century the problem we have to contend with is the conceit of globalization. I say this because with ongoing globalized encounters, more and more local, Indigenous, and racialized communities are being marginalized. Specifically, their/our concerns over self-determination, economic, cultural and political sovereignty, and human dignity are sidelined by the dictates of globalization. Despite the agency and resistance of these groups, they/we are constantly placed in positions of vulnerability. Oppressions and exclusions based on class, gender, sexuality, ability, and race are realities.

Even in so-called industrialized countries food banks and live-in shelters are on the rise as part of invisible homelessness. In our school systems Aboriginal and racialized communities and bodies end up as the victims of systemic neglect and are being "pushed out".

Parts of our educational and other social sector institutions are becoming more and more exclusive and elitist – "Whiter" in terms of culture and knowledge. Issues of "not belonging" hit closer to home for Aboriginal and other disadvantaged groups.

Current trends in knowledge production in a global/transnational context call for critical questions: For example, is claiming Indigenous knowledge and Indigeneity about contradictory ideas and uncritical glorifications of the past? What are the contributions of Indigenous knowledges today in a global/transnational world? How do we translate a pan-Indigenous idea to the local levels of community aspirations? Is the claiming of Indigeneity synonymous to being caught inside the dungeon of Western imperialist knowledge production? Is claiming Indigenous knowledge in the Western academy a centring of Western ideological interests as the basis for human development and social thought? What are the possibilities of a renaissance of Indigenous social thought? What can we do with neo-imperialist forces and internal colonialists who would want to compromise the integrity of Indigenous social thought through Eurocentric mimicry? How has the political and intellectual reclamation of Indigeneity changed the course of Indigenous peoples' relationships with other marginalized communities, including relations with[in] the Diaspora? Where and what are the places of Diasporian social thought within a new pan-Indigenous ideology? While this chapter does not presume to have answers for these important questions, it is significant that we begin our discussion with some understanding of the purpose and scholarly politics of claiming Indigeneity and producing Indigenous knowledge. Fully aware that we may have a right to ask the tough questions, we should have no illusions about getting or expecting the answers we want. These must be achieved through collective negotiation and shared responsibility.

7.3 Situating the "Political Project": Our Collective Responsibility

I may be an idealist, but I believe we must dare to dream. Allow me to take the liberty to ask some emotional and personal questions – key questions that so many of our Elders are usually getting at: How do we practice what we learn? How do we walk the talk? How do we Indigenize our "Other" of Indigenous knowledges, the University? How do we foster the next generation of Indigenous students and scholars?

As enthused in Dei (2008), I have many expectations for the young researchers in the field of Indigenous Studies. Like a number of us in the room, I have encountered many students in my short academic life who have taught and inspired me even as they readily concede my influence on their work. In fact, I owe the inspiration for this discussion to a former student of Hawaiian descent, Leilani Holmes, who teaches at a community college in California and is writing a book on Indigenous Hawaiian knowledge. She is one of those students a teacher comes into contact with and never forgets because of her positive influence. She sent me this note:

> I feel that what you did, George, by connecting our little group at OISE, by always citing our work, by offering us ways to share as co-presenters with you at conferences... all that went beyond the usual graduate school mentoring. Whenever possible you did away with hierarchical thinking and treated us as colleagues and people. And that kind of thing is what this next generation needs and deserves......That is what will help this next generation to build the paths that can become more well-traveled over time – the paths that lead from community to university and back again to community (Personal Communication. Received, April 9, 2007)

Our descendants are our future. I believe this is true for Indigenous knowledge and Indigenous Studies. The coming generation of Indigenous Studies scholars bodes well for the field of education. Conferences need to create platforms and connections for students and established scholars to talk about our experiences. We need sharing and mentoring circles where students and "Elder" scholars act as listeners and mentors, assisting students as they discuss their work, hardships, successes, and failures. All too often at conferences scholars just "take the platform". The younger ones become "satellites", circling around the "stars" in the academic hierarchy. In their rooms, restaurants, and bars our students discuss the disconnect that they feel when there is no path from their home or community to the place they have come to learn.

Most of us working in the field of Indigenous knowledge do so from within universities and other institutions of higher education. Within our institutions production of knowledge is institutionalized on a "production-line" model. In examining Indigenous knowledge we must begin to think through the primary values that live in Indigenous communities. For example, there are ethical precepts or "must-dos". We must ask – How shall we transform the institutions within which we reside? How shall we actively reproduce those core Indigenous values? What is the sense of sharing Indigenous knowledge if it does not work to transform the institutions within which we work and the societies within which we live? How is it ethical to work on Indigenous knowledges all the while replicating hierarchical institutionalized structures and interactional patterns? While these questions are not new, they are not the questions that we have taken to heart!

Academics/scholars/activists working in the area of Indigenous knowledge cannot be stuck in power plays against one another, nor against colleagues in other fields of study. We can ill afford not to speak to one another in our encounters whether on the hallways, in print, or at conferences. We cannot work from a 'scarcity paradigm' in our relentless search for grant money and the next publication. In our work on Indigenous knowledges, we must have time to leave the political economy of knowledge production in the academy "to go outside, into nature, which is at the core of Indigenous knowledge" (Personal Communication. Received, April 9, 2007: 2). Indigenous scholars should lead the way to break free of the production line of publications, teaching, or office hours. Because of the university-style production of knowledge, we often fail to just talk or let knowledge come to us! Our younger scholars – our students – cannot be ignored. We cannot be caught in the crossfire of political battles.

We must Indigenize our institutions. In my role as a recent department Chair I have often asked how I can Indigenize the Department to produce an improved sense of community. It has not been easy but we must keep trying. I believe Indigenous scholars and scholarship can point to important ways. We must always bring the Indigenized values of forgiveness, spiritual healing, and righteousness of praxis into our workplaces. We may not agree with our colleagues but we need to forgive, help, and care for our collective selves. We have to let go of our difficult histories and be forgiving. This is the only way we can live with our Indigenous values where we work. I believe that this is what our Indigenous Elders have talked about and taught us – forgiveness. What good would it do, really, if we continue to write about their "talk" and yet we, as Indigenous scholars and allies, do not bother to try to "walk the talk of our Elders"?

In my experience working in the Western academy, I have come to understand how the "soft" and "sensitive" and "dedicated" students can feel so lost and fragile that they can sometimes just leave – just "fall through the cracks" in the fragmented universe of the university. Sometimes, there are words that lead our students to drop out of their studies. Ironically, those words are usually not about the student's work. They are often just the offhanded comments that both students and instructors make to marginalize others who do not "fit in". Is it enough that our programmes are left with the students who de-Indigenize themselves, de-personalize/disembody the process, or who manage to "toughen up" when marginalized by other students and instructors?

It is only when we start from the position of self-reflexivity that our critiques of the academy can hold sway. African American African-centred theorist Molefi Asante (1999) speaks of the necessary but painful demise of Eurocentrism. This demise holds the possibilities for an end to what Maulana Karenga has called "Europe's self congratulatory conception of itself" (2007b: A9; see also Karenga 1999). There are times when I, as an Indigenous scholar, have not been bold enough to assert my Indigenous scholarship and philosophies in the academy. For sure, it is not for want of trying. However, I marvel at our attempts to mimic Eurocentric thoughts and ideas and often slip into the form, logic, and implicit assumptions of the very things we are contesting. How do we speak about "academic excellence" in a contemporary era remarkable for its celebration of difference and multicentric ways of knowing? How can our institutions claim any intellectual credibility in the face of a dismissal of some ways of knowing? What are the possibilities of community and social engagement that will create a degree of relevance for our academic institutions?

The adaptability, vitality, and agency of Indigenous knowledges open the horizon of human thought, practice, action, and possibilities. These knowledges are reflective of the humility of knowing and respect our viewpoints and cosmologies. Indigenous knowledges embody the essence of ancestral knowings as well as the legacies of diverse histories and cultures. Indigenous knowledges are "speaking back" to the production, categorization, and positioning of cultures, identities, and histories. These knowledges challenge the conventional discursive frameworks and practices that present seemingly unquestionable "truths" about social existence. Indigenous knowledges are about unraveling systemic power relations that have assured the dominance of particular ways of knowing in the academy. In effect, Indigenous knowledges are about resistance, refusal, and transformation. Such knowledges are about the reclamation of the spiritual and ethical traditions of shared interests and concerns, mutual care, social responsibility, equity, and justice. Scholars and learners have an obligation to reaffirm and honour our Indigenous and Aboriginal identities and the remarkable legacies of our ancestral knowledges.

7.4 Indigenous Knowledge: Towards a Conceptualization and Operationalization

Professor Nakata (2007: 12) asked, How do we "establish Indigenous Studies as a discipline, with its own practices for engaging with and testing knowledge"? He noted the expansive territory covered by the global discourse on 'Indigenous Knowledge' as spanning,

....across a range of interests such as sustainable development, bio-diversity and conservation interests, commercial and corporate interests, and Indigenous interests. It circulates at international, national, state, regional, and local levels in government, non-government, and Indigenous community sectors, and across a range of intellectual, public, private, and Indigenous agendas. It is dispersed across various clusters of Western intellectual activity such as scientific research, documentation and knowledge management, intellectual property protection, education, and health. It is politically, economically, and socially implicated in the lives of millions of people around the globe (2).

Indigenous knowledge contrasts with the international knowledge system generated by universities, research institutions, and private firms. Indigenous knowledge – acting as the foundation throughout rural Africa – acts as the basis for local-level decision making in agriculture, health care, food preparation, education, natural resource management, and other activities in rural communities. Today it is asserted that "the current interest in Indigenous Knowledge is emerging at a different historical moment where Indigenous peoples are much better positioned within the legal-political order where issues of rights, sovereignty, self-determination, and historical redress provide a better base for the assertion of Indigenous interests" (Nakata 2007).

In a relatively recent work (Dei and Asgharzadeh 2006) we follow the pioneering works of Fals Borda (1980, 1991) Brokensha et al. (1995), Warren et al. (1995), Agrawal (1995a, b), and Roberts (1998) to conceptualize "Indigenous knowledge" as a way of knowing developed by local/Indigenous peoples over generations as a result of sustained occupation of or attachment to a place, location, or space. This occupancy allows peoples/communities to develop a perfect understanding of the relationship of their communities to their surrounding natural and social environments. Perhaps it is Roberts' (1998: 59) conception of "Indigenous knowledge" as knowledge "accumulated by a group of people, not necessarily Indigenous, who by centuries of unbroken residence develop an in-depth understanding of their particular place in their particular world" that is more telling. Such conceptualization opens the door to multiple forms of Indigenous knowings.

These knowledges share a lot in common: they have emerged in the immediate context of the livelihoods of local peoples as products of a sustained process of creative thought and action within communities when local peoples struggle to deal with "ever changing set of conditions and problems" (Agrawal 1995b: 5). Such knowledge is dynamic, undergoing constant modifications as peoples and communities negotiate their complex relations with nature, land, culture, and society. Indigenous knowledge is relevant to the extent that it addresses the needs of the community. While this knowledge is localized and context-bound, it does not mean that it can be Boxed in time and space, nor does it transcend boundaries. All knowledges are in constant motion; and the fluidity of interactions of different knowledges makes every knowledge dynamic. Purcell (1998: 266) also points out that "as colonialism uprooted Indigenous peoples it also uprooted their knowledge systems." However, these knowledge systems have continued over centuries to adjust to and persist in new environments. The recognition of the specific situatedness of knowledge forms does not amount to a "fetishization of the local" (Ginsburg 1994: 366).

Referring to African and other Indigenous contexts, local proverbs, parables, fables, mythologies, and folklore contain words of wisdom, instruction, and knowledge about society as sources of Indigenous cultural knowings. These expressions of the traditions and histories of diverse groups offer critical understandings of the complex inter-weavings of society, nature, and culture. They teach about communal belonging, responsibility, and purpose. They support "learning as community", learners' rights and responsibilities, and learning as a cooperative and collaborative undertaking. Proverbs, parables, fables, mythologies, and folklore are rich sources of knowledge that sustain communities and validate human experiences. Through oral traditions, these bodies of knowledge have been passed down from generation to generation (Dei and Asgharzadeh 2006).

In conceptualizing Indigenous knowledges, certain issues must be broached. We must challenge binarisms and dualistic modes of thought. For example, we ought to seek to destabilize any conceptions of Indigenous *or* Western systems of knowledge as "good" or "bad" knowledge. We must evoke Indigenous knowledge to challenge the linearity of Western paradigms privileged in the academy. In this regard, the power of thinking in circles can release us from linear modes of thought and the culture of knowledge hierarchies. Our conceptions of Indigeneity must also challenge static conceptions of "Indigenous". Despite the pitfalls, limitations, and costs, we can still cultivate an Indigenous space in the Western academy. This space can empower a synthesis or "cultural interface" of knowledge. We must move Indigenous knowledge from its contexts and place it on a different terrain. This is the idea of "Indian/Aboriginal/Indigenous removal"– putting Indigenous knowledge "onto the reserve". This metaphor has real implications. I do not want to see Indigenous knowledge placed in a particular "space" within the academy.

Sometimes, the "spoken word" cannot survive the passage of time and must be textualized. Yet, we must uphold the power of orality as an elegant and purposeful form of knowledge-making. We must challenge and resist the appropriation and commodification of Indigenous knowledge forms. Indigenous knowledge derives from collective experience and actions. The tensions of filtering such collective dimensions of knowledge through a highly individualistic and competitive academy are real and consequential.

Bringing a humility of knowing and acknowledging the power of the "not knowing" are critical components of Indigeneity. They form part of the whole discourse about the sacredness of activity. Such sacred activity allows our knowledges speak to others.

Not all knowledges are indigenous to particular locations and communities. I would argue that we must be careful in ascribing 'Indigeneity' to all knowledge systems. Similarly, Indigenous knowledges are not homogenous. They are demarcated by regional, class, ethnic, gender, and religious differences. In fact, all knowledges are social and political creations serving specific interests. But we cannot idealize the "difference of knowledges". There is interplay and exchange among and between cultures and communities; it is this process that harmonizes difference within local communities and their knowledges. While there may be significant intellectual, cultural, and political disagreements within communities, important lines of connection can, nonetheless, develop across group boundaries and Indigenous communities with implications for knowledge systems.

7.5 Politics of Identity and the Search for Epistemological Equity

In my ongoing research on equity and questions of epistemology with graduate student researchers, we are bringing another level of interrogation to Indigenous knowledges. The question of how to create spaces where multiple knowledges can co-exist in the Western academy is central, especially so since Eurocentric knowledge subsumes and appropriates other knowledges without crediting sources. At issue is the search for epistemological equity. In fact, Indigeneity and Indigenous knowledge are about the search for epistemological equity. We all know there are different conceptions. One of my colleagues, Tanya Titchkosky, claims that equity is not something one simply possesses; rather, it is something we must collectively work to achieve. We must set goals, identify and remove the myriad barriers that lie in our way and engage in enduring struggle. There are tensions between how we come to operationalize equity and equality. Equality is about levelling the playing field. In contrast, equity is about responding specifically to the exclusion of certain bodies. This response may not necessarily entail equalizing the playing field. It may mean much more for praxis.

We must attend to the ontological and epistemological claims of Indigenous knowings. In order to breathe life into equity, we must situate equity in discussions over Indigenous knowledge production and Indigeneity. Epistemological equity is contingent on recognizing subject identities as "real" and consequential.

Identities thrive under particular material and discursive conditions. Therefore, caution must be exercised when becoming dismissive of identity politics. Identity politics have in recent years been held in disrepute and, rather disturbingly, literally prosecuted to death. But identity politics is neither vulgar nor irrelevant. How can we afford to ignore the consequences of misrecognition of self and subject identities? Identities can provide the foundations of structural critique when the pursuit of politics is located or grounded in one's positionality. We need to ask who gets to claim their identities, for whom, how, and for what purposes? The negation of identity can be a form of selective historical amnesia when we come to think of how certain identities have been encoded with punishment, while others have been privileged throughout history.

Theorizing must lead to politics. The worth of a "social theory" must not be measured simply in terms of its philosophical and ontological claims but in terms of the ability of theory to offer social and political correctives. In speaking about theorizing "Indigeneity" and "Aboriginality", I want to take back theory and make it work to reflect one's politics and lived realities. Knowledge, experience, and practice must lead to theory. Consequently, as Indigenous and Aboriginal peoples, we cannot theorize ourselves out of our identities.

In fact, not to speak of identity/ies may be a luxury for some. It is a luxury because its denial is "costless" when it is a denial of privilege. For many to deny a racial, class, gender, sexuality, ability, or even spiritual identity is unthinkable. Such identities are real and have consequences in everyday experience. Identity is about who we are, our social locations, and how we come to know and act politically.

No one today comes out openly to say that Indigenous knowledges are "beneath the dignity of the Western academy". Yet, there is little doubt that there exists a scepticism towards Indigenous knowledge and the claims to know from an Indigenous experience. When do we, as Indigenous peoples and scholars, get to say who we are outside of the Euro-centred hegemonic construction of our identities? How do we establish the Indigenous presence in our institutions? I would argue that perhaps we do so through claims to identity, place, and culture. What we make of the Indigenous presence also depends on the extent to which we as Indigenous scholars and workers use our collective identities to organize politically and intellectually for change. What makes our institutions a successful place for Indigenous/Aboriginal and racial minority learners is our ability to resist marginalization and to claim a space. This is a constant struggle. Once we claim our space it is even more difficult to hold on to that space.

Let me allude briefly and metaphorically to Indigenous bodies and the land, and Indigenous minds and the university. Indigenous struggles to hold onto our lands – to keep our land-based sovereignty – are mirrored in Indigenous struggles to hold onto our knowledges – to keep our intellectual sovereignty. In the Canadian educational context, the brick walls of our universities evoke the red brick walls of Aboriginal residential schools. The forced removal of Indigenous bodies replicates itself in the continual displacement of Indigenous knowledge. A colonial hierarchy of knowledge in the university ensures that Indigenous minds, experiences, and subjectivities are discounted. Our presence is a daily struggle against invisibility. We live in a perpetual state of resistance. For every constructed Universal "Us" in the academy there is an Excluded "Other" – and the "Other" is the Indigenous "Us".

The voice of difference holds a power that I have termed "epistemic saliency" as it circulates through debates about oppression, colonialization, and Indigeneity. The experiences of oppression/colonization position us to know differently as we unpack the dynamics of oppression and Indigeneity.

Our histories and identities are unique and yet contingent and intertwined. The uniqueness of Aboriginal histories and existence necessitates a conceptual and practical distinction of issues affecting Aboriginal communities and those of other racialized communities. This does not mark our knowledge more relevant or valid but does affirm that the connection of identities to knowledge production should not lead to a form of "epistemic relativism". The contingent and intertwined nature of our histories and identities means that Indigeneity and anti-racism may be pursued in ways that create divisions and binaries between concerns of Aboriginality and racialization of subjects.

In the Euro-American context, while I agree that the Aboriginal bodies experience a separate and distinct kind of racism, this form of racism is in a great part related to their identities. For example, what does Indian-ness mean? In other words, anti-Indianness as a virulent form of racism is different and yet connected to anti-Black/African racism. The epistemological and pedagogical understandings of oppressions point to powerful connections of racisms and Aboriginal colonization, imperialism, and cultural genocide. We need to consider how the voices of the Middle Passage, to cite one emblematic example, are or are not heard and given space within the classroom. Are their stories honoured? Or, as does happen all too often, silenced?

Bodies matter in discourses about Indigeneity. This is a question of transcendence. This is beyond a project of representation, linking identity to knowledge production and/or the idea of multiple knowings. The idea of embodied knowing draws a connection between identity and knowledge production. More importantly, claiming Indigeneity is about spiritual healing and praxis that calls for an embodiment of knowledge. In evoking notions of the "spiritual" in the politics of claiming Indigeneity, we also look for ways to deal with the despiritualization of the "self" – the disconnection between soul, mind, and body in conventional knowledge production.

7.6 Towards a Critical Indigenous Discursive Framework

In this section of the chapter, I want to propose some ideas and principles for the development of a critical framework of Indigeneity to meet contemporary challenges (see also Dei 2008). I ground this undertaking in an African knowledge base. I am working with Indigenous African concepts, values, and principles: community, collective responsibility, mutual interdependence, and responsible governance. This knowledge base, not unique to African peoples or cultures, is shared by most Indigenous communities. However, the Indigenous discursive framework I propose also incorporates Diasporan social thought. It has a broader project of decolonization, one that conjoins the mental, spiritual, political, and material levels. However, I place spirituality, rather than politics or economics, at the centre of the analysis.

I argue that the search for Indigenousness is only a means to an end, especially as Indigenous peoples claim discursive power. I feel compelled to reiterate that in recent years we hear of such discourses as "New Humanism" and a "Renaissance". The Indigenous contributions to global humanity and world civilization have been long-standing. There is nothing new about that humanism. Indigenous knowledge is old, and the Western concept of Humanism takes its cue from Indigenity. I have an identical response to the word "renaissance" – another trope that has such a Western heritage.

The framework roots Indigenous identity within history but outside Euro-American hegemonic constructions of the Other. It empowers us to reframe our Indigenous histories as we navigate the current diasporic context. The framework projects a cultural rebirth and revival reflecting the integrity and pride in self, culture, history, and heritage, as well as a commitment to the collective good and well-being of all peoples. The ideas and principles of an Indigenous discursive framework are rooted and actionable in local/grassroots political organizing and as a form of intellectual activism. Discursively this framework affirms a local, national, and international consciousness and an understanding of the politics of "national culture and liberation" that is matched with political sophistication and intricacies.

I now put forward the thirteen (13) principles by way of offering a conceptual and analytical clarification of the critical Indigenous discursive framework:

a) Land, history, culture, and identity have powerful explanatory powers in contemporary communities and socio-political encounters.
b) History, culture, and spiritual identity are sites and sources of asymmetrical power relations structured along the lines of difference, including race, class, gender, sexuality, [dis]ability, and culture.
c) Land and spiritual identity are salient, fundamental analytical concepts offering an entry point in understanding the lived experiences of those who are Indigenized.
d) Recognize that "land and spiritual identity" have special salience that should not lead us to a discourse of reductionism or the idea of essentialized difference.
e) Land and spiritual identity achieve their full effect when intersected with class, gender, sexuality, [dis]Ability, language, and culture.
f) A critical Indigenous discursive framework brings three (3) conceptual understandings to Indigeneity: (i) colonialism, in its deep-reaching denial of history and identity, has created unequal outcomes for groups in terms of their histories and spiritual identities; (ii) emergence of different identities; (iii) the urgency of regaining their spiritual power and strength.
g) The power of Western knowledge rests on its epistemological racism', built on the assumptions of the superiority of Western civilization (Scheurich and Young 1999). Indigenous knowing resists the dominance of the West and its power to subsume all forms of thought, with notions like – "reason", "progress", "rationality", and the "Enlightened discourse".
h) Power within Western cultures and knowledges exists in hierarchies. Such hierarchies of power are themselves only meaningful in a competitive culture. The competitive nature of these communities helps to produce "Othered subjects".
i) It is through a nurturing of oppositional stances, ones informed by our relative subject positions and experiences, that the dominance of the West and Eurocentricty can be subverted. In fact, the Indigenous discursive framework claims the intellectual agency of the Indigene to define herself and to set the terms of engagement in dominant culture.
j) A critical Indigenous discursive framework is anti-colonial. It is about resistance, subject[ive] agency, and collective politics. It centres the agency, voice, and political and intellectual interests of Indigenous and Aboriginal subjects in accounting and resisting oppression and domination. The politics of knowledge production for Indigenous and Aboriginal scholars claims agency through self-actualization and collective empowerment.
k) The Indigenous discursive approach poses alternative conceptions of "difference" and "Otherness". It challenges the notion of social difference as a "problem", seeing an important distinction between affirming difference and engaging in a politics of "Otherness". A "theory of difference" constructs

difference as a site of identities, knowledge, and power; while a "theory of Otherness" constructs difference as the negative "Other". The process of Othering establishes "self/Other" – "us/we" distinctions – and provides a basis for denying resources and power to groups in society. Otherness imagines difference simply in the exotic Other rather than seeing difference as an embodiment of knowledge, power, and subjective agency.

l) The Indigenous discursive framework highlights spirituality and spiritual ontology. This calls for placing the "spiritual" at the centre of social movement politics, making questions of culture and history the superstructure. This approach to Indigenous praxis extends beyond being a project of decolonization to unravelling of the power relations of knowledge production, interrogation, valid tion, and dissemination.

m) Finally, the Indigenous discursive framework critiques independent "scholarship", "politics", and "activism". It does not subscribe to the luxury of the independence of scholarship from politics and activism. But the framework is also mindful of not dictating a particular politics. The learning objective is to create a space to legitimize politics in the intellectual/academic realm.

The Indigenous discursive framework centralizes the notion of spirituality and spiritual ontology. The spiritual is a valid way of knowing. Spirituality is about reflection. Spirituality is contested and resisted; it also about body, mind and soul interface. Spirituality is also about relationships and dialogue with one inner self and a community. Spiritual epistemology is about a spiritual way of knowing that centers the inner self/environment and make connections with the outer group/environment. There is the power of a spiritual dialogue and spirituality cannot be discussed outside the context of power (e.g. imposition of spiritual beliefs; suppression of spiritual connections; the power of what spirituality does for oneself. The Indigenous discursive framework only moves beyond a conception of spirituality as individual, personal and unique to the subject. It is important to reiterate that religion and spirituality while in separable are not coterminous and the discursive framework being posited here acknowledges that one can be religious and yet lack a spiritual core. In articulating a *spiritual ontology* I do recognize the importance of having a spiritual community with a communal ontology. The theoretical grounding of such spiritual ontology also links human identity to the space of nature/natural, culture and society.

There is a practice of silence as a form of resistance, that is, resisting concepts/ideas. But silence can also be a spiritual engagement, that is, as a form of contemplation and reflection. We must see spirituality as beyond dualities, beyond the physical and material. Claims of spirituality avoid splitting of the self. Colonizing education/colonial knowledge production has always presented social phenomena as structural accounts/forms, thereby downplaying the human element/dimensions of emotions and intuition. In the era of perpetual secularization of our communities, we fail to express and bring a deeper meaning to life and our existence. That hegemonic discourse that denigrates and devalues other ways of knowings also allows the colonized and minoritized to seek affirmation and legitimation in the norms/values and ideas of such hegemonic knowings. There is a need to create a path of spiritual recovery from the "spirit injury" and depersonalization of selves and the amputation of a part of one's humanity (e.g. history/culture). Having a spiritual identity is also about a moral and political identity.

7.7 Indigenous Knowledges Today: Pedagogic Possibilities for Anti-colonial Education

Allow me to move into the notion of anti-colonial education and its pedagogical possibilities. Indigenous knowledge is part of the struggle for self-determination and political and intellectual sovereignty of Indigenous peoples. Claiming Indigenous knowledge in the Western academy is part of an anti-colonial struggle for independence from exploitative relations of schooling and knowledge production. To the critical learner, the strength of Indigeneity lies in the synergies of culture, history, and identity. Scholarship and politics of education should first seek the intellectual wellness and improvement of the person and personhood of each learner.

In reclaiming Indigeneity, scholarship must connect firmly with Indigenous struggles and aspirations. For example, the history and culture of the Indigenous peoples are part of political, material, spiritual, and mental decolonization. The search for knowledge is valuable, if it allows Indigenous peoples to identify with their histories, cultures, identities, and land. An Indigenous framework, with its interconnections of self, group, community, culture, and nature, offers compelling arguments against racism, colonialism, and imperialism that have ensured divisions, fragmentation, and inequities in communities. Indigenous peoples' survival and destiny rests on a form of intellectual, cultural, spiritual, and political liberation and emancipation grounded in an anti-colonial modernity (Du Bois 1947).

In the search for solutions to current social problems, the relevance of Indigenous concepts and practices is not in doubt. In fact, the pedagogical possibilities of Indigenous knowledges point to three major areas in need of interrogation.

First, there is the need to reclaim Indigenous past, history, culture, and spiritual identities for knowledge production. This implies a resistance to amputation and offering an intellectual challenge to those who would subjugate Indigenous peoples' knowings and experiences. Indigenous knowledge is about culture and rootedness in place and history.

Second, there is the search for an understanding of the possibilities of anti-colonial education. Anti-colonial education is about challenging contemporary forms of post-colonial education as vestiges of "neo-colonial brainwashing" (Chinweizu 2007). Such education continues to denigrate what Indigenous peoples and their cultures have to offer the world. We, as Indigenous scholars and activists, must continually work to find ways to address the [ir]relevance of school curriculum, texts, classrooms, pedagogy, and instructional strategies. Anti-colonial education must also address social difference.

We must rethink the post-colonial education project of national integration, citizenship responsibility, and nation building. My research work on African schooling and education (Dei and Asgharzadeh 2006), for example, reveals that the goals of national integration, post-independence, and "post-colonial" education in Africa often deny heterogeneity in local populations. It is as if difference itself is a problem. With this orientation, education has undoubtedly helped create and maintain the glaring disparities and inequities, structured along lines of ethnicity, culture, language, religion, ability, sexuality, gender, and class, which persist and grow. This pattern must be disrupted. An anti-colonial education will bring an expansive definition to colonial and colonizing relations as anything that is "imposed and dominating".

The question of identity connects issues of Indigeneity and belonging in terms of a rootedness in a place and culture. In Canadian contexts there are obviously current re-articulations of "nation", "citizenship", and "belonging" that reveal the complexities of subjective identities and politics. Youth culture and diasporic identities exemplify these complexities. But apart from youth born in the diasporic contexts, there are others (including their parents) who still trace their rootedness to particular ancestral homelands. As members of the "nation" and "communities", the experiences of these individuals cannot be denied even as we seek to privilege new youth identities in the nation. These adults are not displaced, nor can they be seduced into amputating their past. Furthermore, the world is not just about the diasporic encounter, nor is the cosmopolitan the only place of abode and meaning. The connection here is that Indigenous peoples need to listen to the voice of the Diaspora which is differently inflected for the youth. Youthful versus Elder Indigenous voices offer different insights, ones we must listen to as youth negotiate the terrains of the Diaspora, migration, and multiply located identities.

Anti-colonial education must begin to theorize the 'Indigenous' beyond its current boundaries and spatialization. For so-called "displaced" or migrated communities, the search for diasporic connections must not only lead to a gaze on the ruptures, disruptions, or discontinuities. This search must also promote claims of belonging and connectedness to place, identities, and cultures. In the latter sense, I am making reference to connecting Indigeneity to contemporary issues such as racism and colonial oppressions, ableism, women's rights, gays and lesbian rights, patriarchy, AIDS/Health, environment, classism, and poverty.

One of the biggest pedagogical challenges of anti-colonial education is the search for the synthesis of multiple knowledges. As Nakata (2007) reminds us, some scholars dispute the importance of this synthesis. Some take the position that Indigenous knowledge systems and Western sciences are "so disparate as to be 'incommensurable'" (Verran 2005) or "irreconcilable" (Russell 2005) on "cosmological, epistemological and ontological grounds" (Nakata 2007: 2). Sometimes the maker of difference is in what is deemed "science" and "not science" or what is "valid" knowledge and what is "not valid" and the criterion for making these determinations. We must search for connecting points of different and multiple knowledges. Nakata (2007) cautions that:

> ... it is important for those wanting to bring Indigenous knowledge into teaching and learning contexts to understand what happens when Indigenous Knowledge is conceptualised simplistically and oppositionally from the standpoint of scientific paradigms as everything

that is 'not science'. It is also important to understand what happens when Indigenous knowledge is documented in ways that disembodies it from the people who are its agents, when the 'knowers' of that knowledge are separated out from what comes to be 'the known', in ways that dislocates it from its locale, and separates it from the social institutions that uphold and reinforce its efficacy, and cleaves it from the practices that constantly renew its meanings in the here and now (5).

Of course, we cannot pursue synthesis while failing to recognize the pitfalls, limits, and the perils. We need to remind and ask ourselves: what is the politics of creating a knowledge synthesis? In articulating the meanings of "the cultural interface" and the possibilities of forging a critical Indigenous standpoint, as Nakata (2007) notes, "I am not out singularly to overturn the so-called dominant position through simplistic arguments of omission, exclusion or misrepresentation but rather out there to make better arguments in relation to my position within knowledge, and in relation to other communities of 'knowers'. We see and act on things in these ways all the time" (11). Far from being simplistic, however, I do believe pointing to the omissions, negations, and devaluations are politically and intellectually important. The omissions, negations, and erasures are relevant to the politics of legitimizing multiple knowledges in the academy, as well as exposing the tendency for some forms of knowing to masquerade as universal even when they are borrowing from other ways of knowing.

Synthesis of different knowledge has always been an important aspect of Indigenous philosophies and ontologies. Discursive synthesis is at the heart of claims of multicentric knowing. Connections of ideas to different spaces and locales have been recognized in Indigenous thought processes and expressions. In fact, the notions of "humility of knowing" and "uncertainty of knowledge" imply that the learner must always welcome multiple interpretations of social events, facts, and ideas given the location, politics, and identities of the learner as knower.

I conclude where I began by claiming the power of the humility of knowing and an awareness of the existence of multiple meanings, interpretations, and experiences. Rather than seeking to offer definitive definitions or models of Indigenous scholarship, this discussion makes its case for the salience of these ways of knowing. The next chapter considers some of the real-world implications as we move from theory and advocacy to the provision of real-world education.

References

Agrawal, A. (1995a) Dismantling the Divide Between Indigenous and Western Knowledge. *Development and Change*, 26(3), 413–439.

Agrawal, A. (1995b) Indigenous and Scientific Knowledge: Some Critical Comments. *Indigenous Knowledge and Development Monitor*, 3(3), 3–5.

Asante, M. (1999) *The Painful Demise of Eurocentrism: An African-Centred Response to Critics*. Trenton, NJ: Africa World Press.

Brokensha, D., D. M. Warren, and Werner, O. (Eds.) (1995) *Indigenous Knowledge Systems and Development*. Boston: University Press of America.

Chinweizu, W. (2007). Black Colonialist: The Root of the Trouble in Nigeria. An Achebe Foundation Interview of Chinweizu by Paul Odidi.

Dei, G. J. S. (2008) Indigenous Knowledge Studies and the Next Generation: Pedgogical Possibilities for Anti-Colonial Education. *Australian Journal of Indigenous Education*, 37, 5–13.

Dei, G. J. S. and Asgharzadeh, A. (2006) Indigenous Knowledges and Globalization: An African Perspective. In Abdi, A., Puplampu, K. and Dei, G. (Eds.) *African Education and Globalization: Critical Perspectives* (pp. 53–78). Lanham, MD: Lexington Books.

Du Bois, W. E. B. (1947) *The World and Africa*. New York: Viking Press.

Fals Borda, O. (1980) *Science and the Common People*. Yugoslvia: Sarajevo.

Fals-Borda, O. (1991) Some Basic Ingredients. In Fals-orda, O. and Rahman, M. A. (Eds.) *Action and Knowledge: Breaking the Monopoly with Participatory Action-Research* (pp. 3–12). New York: The Apex Press.

Ginsburg, F. (1994) Embedded Aesthetics: Creating Discursive Space for Indigenous Media. *Cultural Anthropology*, 9(3), 365–382.

Karenga, M. (1999) Whiteness Studies: Deceptive or Welcome Discourse?. *Black Issues in Higher Education*, 16(6), 26–28.

Karenga, M. (2007b) The Flawed Foundation of America: Jamestown and Herrenvolk Democracy. *Los Angeles Sentinel*. February 22, p. A9.

Nakata, M. (2007). The Cultural Interface. *The Australian Journal of Indigenous Education*, 36(5), 2–14.

Pohlhaus, G. (2002) Knowing Communities: An Investigation of Harding's Standpoint Epistemology. *Social Epistemology*, 16(3), 283–293.

Purcell, T. W. (1998) Indigenous Knowledge and Applied Anthropology: Question of Definition and Direction. *Human Organization*, 57(3), 258–272.

Roberts, M. (1998). Indigenous Knowledge and Western Science: Perspectives from the Pacific. In D. Hodson (Ed.) *Science and Technology Education and Ethnicity: An Aoteroa/New Zealand Perspective* (pp. 59–75). Proceedings of a conference held at the Royal Society of New Zealand, Thorndon, Wellington, May 7–8, 1996. The Royal Society of New Zealand Miscellaneous Series #50.

Russell, L. (2005) Indigenous Knowledge and the Archives: Accessing Hidden History and Understandings. In Nakata, M. and Langton, M. (Eds.) *Australian Indigenous Knowledge and Libraries*. Kingston, Australia: Australian Academic & Research Libraries, Australian Library and Information Association.

Scheurich, J. and Young, M. (1999) Coloring Epistemologies. *Educational Researcher*, 26(4), 4–16.

Verran, H. (2005). "Knowledge traditions of Aboriginal Australians: Questions and Answers Arising in a Databasing Project", Draft published by Making Collective Memory with Computers. School of Australian Indigenous Knowledge Systems, Charles Darwin University, Darwin, Northern Territory. http://www.cdu.ed.au/centres/ik/pdf/knowledgeanddatabasing.pdf

Warren, D. M., Slikkerveer, L. J., and Brokensha, D. (Eds.) (1995) *The Cultural Dimension of Development: Indigenous Knowledge Systems*. Exeter: Intermediate Technology Publications.

Wente, M. (2007) Is This Woman An Islamophobe?. *Globe and Mail*. March 31, 2007, p. A25.

Chapter 8
Politicizing the Contemporary Learner: Implications for African Schooling and Education

Abstract As part of its advocacy for African-centred and, more generally, equitable schooling, this discussion proposes a selection of effective student engagement strategies. Seeking to engage educators and students in a dialogue about the lessons learned from existing African-focused schools in the United States, this chapter also provides insights about how to learn from the challenges and successes of these programmes.

Keywords Politicization · Contemporary learner · Advocacy · African-centred schooling · Student engagement · Educators · United States · Infused curriculum · Diversity · Responsive school programming

8.1 Introduction: On Identity and Community

I begin this chapter with poignant questions: What can schools teach? How can education help learners navigate critical questions of equity, difference, power, and social responsibility? The answers lie in the possibilities of an educational strategy different from conventionally tolerant multiculturalism. This is a new educational strategy that addresses the following: (a) critical notions of "identity" and "community" in schooling; (b) the power and limits of critical education; and (c) connecting the elements of spirituality, identity, community, and critical education to offer genuine educational options or alternatives.

I share the view that Bhabha's (1994) notions of "hybridity" and the implications for claims of "hybrid identities" are very relevant. Similarly, critiques to do with the constructions and "exoticization" of multiculturalism and cultural diversity are pertinent.

But an equally relevant question is: What are we doing when we trouble notions of "community" and "identity" to render the concepts irrelevant in contemporary social and educational politics?

Hybridity means more than just a collection of multiple identities. It means new combinations, and an end product of something different. But do we end up losing the "original"? In the making of the "new" what happens to the old/past? Is it transformed completely or critically questioned? Is there recourse to past, history, culture, and tradition to solve contemporary problems? As Andrew Lattas (1993: 6) long ago noted, "the present is itself constitute of what is NOT, the past." I say this because of a concern with a wholesale negation or critiques of the "past", "collective identities", and "communities" that denounce the transformative potential of resistance and oppression politics. Are we all cultural hybrids? It is important for an interrogation of "identity" and "community" to affirm the fact that these notions can also be self-consciously claimed for political ends that are not always for causes of violence or extremism.

As Davies notes, "community" and "identity" are not always assigned. Community does not always imply the absence of choice. Community can be claimed, and we must not delegitimize an individual's claim to belong to a particular community. "Communities of difference" are comprised of "communities". The problem with contemporary education is that the schools I know do not necessarily teach about "community" and "identity" in positive ways, as solution-oriented spaces for advocacy, resolving differences, and seeking solutions to social problems. These are the political requirements of "social responsibility" and "belongingness".

Furthermore, what do we do with the propensity of the dominant to claim "fragmented communities" in order to deny accountability and responsibility?

This question leads me to the interrogation of "faith-based schools" and "segregated schools". I have qualms with the term segregation when applied to contemporary schooling initiatives intended to address specific concerns so that education serves the needs of all students. Definitions of segregation are politically loaded. The jargon of the fifties harkens back to issues of discrimination, oppression, and the denial of opportunity and privilege for some and not others.

Davies's assertion that "My view is that segregated schools based on language (such as in Canada or Belgium) pose fewer problems, in that it is possible to see other language speakers as equal. But segregated schools based on belief or ethnicity are a hostage to fortune, and deny on a daily basis attempts at a community humanity."

Those who propose focused schools in Euro-American contexts, notably Black/African-centered focused schools, do not define these schools on the basis of race or ethnicity. These schools, where they exist, do not teach students about their superior status, nor are they taught to see others as "inferior". These schools are intended to address the inferiorization of other marginalized groups by the current school system.

8.2 The Power of "Critical Education"

Critical education can tackle issues of religious fundamentalism and help us move beyond a plea for "respect" and "tolerance" if questions of power, equity, and difference are concretely dealt with. There is a difference between the mere acknowledgement of difference and concretely addressing difference. I see the latter as the surest way to stem the root causes of violence and extremism in schools and society. Notwithstanding good intentions, the problem with peace and citizenship education is that these end up as "liberal approaches" to education that fail to address asymmetrical power relations structured along lines of difference, including race, class, gender, religion, ability, sexuality, and language.

To deal with power and social difference, peace and citizenship education must work with the following three conceptual understandings: (a) relative saliencies of different identities; (b) situational and contextual variations in intensities of oppression and according privilege; and (c) severity of issues for different bodies.

So, while we emphasize complexities, contingencies, multiple realities, and truths, schools must also address the uncritical acceptance of critical education. Rather than being a site for passive socialization, schooling opens possibilities for a critical questioning and rethinking of social relationships, identities, and power.

8.3 Connecting Religion, Identity, Community, and Critical Education: The Search for Educational Options/Alternatives

Part of the problem is that there may in fact be no moral core at the heart of our institutional systems. How do we live with the educational reality that the system is failing many of our youth while having reservations about alternative programmes directed to serve primarily these youth? Public education requires courage to think differently and insist that things be set "right" when we are not always on the "right path". This is an ethical responsibility that reflects the politics of ethicality by calling for concrete action to redress injustice. This is what critical public education should be about.

Public schools need to ask about the ideological, political, and spiritual frameworks that have perpetuated educational and social inequalities. The key challenge is whether we can change the current school system without subverting the entire social system of which it is a part. In other words, schooling and educational transformation are demolition exercises. The current schooling system is the creation and product of a colonial system. Strategies for educational change should be pragmatic if we are to be successful in genuine transformation of schools.

Some forms of alternative schooling are very comfortable with exclusion. Private sector involvement in schooling is a case in point. While private schools have emerged as part of our modern democracies, state disengagement from the public sphere has allowed the latter to determine schooling within a context of corporate global market. The creation of exclusive private spaces in schools has cemented social divides.

There are important intellectual traditions to work with for the promotion of education that truly serves the needs of all students. It is critical in rethinking schooling for educators to read the problem of marginality from different perspectives. We cannot concretely respond to the challenges of schooling and marginality without confronting the question of identity and the links to schooling, social difference, and community knowledge. The tendency to homogenize student populations marginalizes some youth and their communities.

To rethink schooling is to serve the needs of all youth. We must challenge the dominant's sense of entitlement. The success of any educational initiative to enhance students' learning would depend on the extent of teacher preparation, training, and development to address the issues of equity and excellence in education. All educators must develop a higher expectation of every learner. Such expectation will make educators acutely aware of the importance of continually tracking and monitoring students' progress with the object of actually assisting the learner, not just satisfying bureaucratic requirements.

Thus, there is a need for a discursive repositioning in terms of a critical reflection of what teachers do in classrooms and a shift away from the deficit thinking and pathologizing discourses. Culture is central to schooling, classroom teachings, and school interrelations. Educational achievement is the outcome of social interactions in schools involving many actors and subjects. While test scores may be important to determine what is happening to learners, teacher preparation must be geared towards finding ways to measure the effectiveness of the structures and processes of educational delivery. Measurements include levels of culturally responsive teaching that go beyond mere improvement in test scores.

The relationships between teachers and students in the classrooms and school settings have the biggest impact on students' learning. This may run contrary to what some educators perceive as the relations between homes, communities, and students as having the greatest impact on learning. Ways to build positive relationships with students include the following:

a) continue to take time to get to know students, their stories, and their learning needs;
b) expand the walls of the classroom by inviting local experts, including Elders, families, and community activists, to share their stories and experiences with students;
c) diversify the content and format of reading and viewing materials, including sourcing materials from new filmmakers, alternative media, and youth;
d) feature African, Asian, Hispanic, and Aboriginal visuals and songs;
e) create opportunities for student activism and volunteerism within the school and the wider community;
f) work with local farmer's markets to source locally grown fruits and vegetables for a school-to-table food programme, with Recipes reflecting the diversity of the students, to provide ensures healthy and accessible meals for students;
g) go beyond African History or Asian History Month to provide recurring and sustained references to the multiple stories and experiences of our students and their cultures;
h) as a teacher, model your critical thinking skills as you invite students to think about popular culture portrayals of them, their culture, and their community;

i) consider referencing and demonstrating African-centred values, including truth, justice, and balance, in your day-to-day interactions with students, colleagues, and families;
j) advocate for the expansion of curriculum to include a wider range of equity-focused courses, including studies and challenges of ableism, homophobia, classism, and cultural bias.

Some educators are fond of explaining students' underachievement in schools as victims of pathological lifestyles (Dei et al. 1997). The dominant perpetuation of a racialized order can be seen in the low expectations that some educators hold of marginalized youth in schools.

8.4 A Question of Language

Language and marginalization in education are subjects that have received attention in the educational literature, given the realization that language plays a critical role in the education of youth. It is important for educators to see language as an issue of effective educational delivery, comprehension of knowledge, and as an equal opportunity educational issue. Among the critical issues in language and education one can point to the following: (a) the question of the first language of students; (b) standard language of the textbooks used in classroom; (c) language of instruction in schools and classrooms; (d) the language background of educators themselves.

Language diversity is an advantage, a source of strength for a learner, and furthers the goals of schooling and learning. The promotion of children's first languages is a plus for their education. Textbook and classroom transaction in the second language should be comprehensible to children at every stage. Teachers should be bilingual especially where children are themselves of bilingual background. Educational strategies ought to "initiate teaching in children's first language, continue first language development till as late as possible" or develop "flexible approaches to second language acquisition based on local situations" (Jhingram 2007: n.p.).

8.5 African-Centred School and the Moral Panic

My commitment to Africentric schooling is long standing, having both professional and personal significance for me (Dei 1993). On 30 January 2008, the board of trustees of Toronto District School Board (TDSB) voted 11-9 to have an Africentric pilot school. The school opened in September 2009 at the Sheppard Public School to cater for junior Kindergarten to grade 6. There is hope for an extension to high school grades in future years. One of the refreshing things is how the school appears to have exceeded its initial targets and there is mention of a waiting list of parents/guardians wanting to get their children enrolled in the school. This is great and the long struggle has begun to bear some fruits. Clearly, Toronto and Ontario are on the verge of embarking upon an exciting venture which I strongly believe augurs well for the public school system. Contrary to its misinformed critics, I firmly maintain the success of the Africentric School will offer significant lessons for the mainstream public school. There is a long history of community activism in Black education. Regarding the Africentric School in the Canadian context, there is a particular history that is relevant to the trials and tribulations of local parental activism for educational change. We know that in November 1992, a multi-level government task force, the "African-Canadian Community Working Group", proposed that one predominantly Black junior high school should be set up in each of the six metropolitan Toronto municipalities. The 15-member working group was appointed by the four levels of government – federal, provincial, City of Toronto, and Metro Toronto (Working Group 1992). Together with a series of other recommendations, the report suggested a five-year pilot scheme, establishing a Black-focused institution (African-centered school) where Black history and culture would be taught. The earlier proponents were influenced by our (African scholars and educators) existing writings on the subject. It was also clear the success of Saturday schools in enriching the learning for African-Canadian youth was not lost on these proponents.

Then, in 1994, the Royal Commission on Learning (also set up by the Ontario provincial government) after extensive consultations with educators, researchers, students, parents and policy makers also recommended setting up "demonstrated schools" along the same lines at the Working Group's recommendation to deal with the problem of African-Canadian youth "underachievement" (RCOL 1994). I recall as a member of the Organization of Parents of Black Children (OPBC) contributing to a collective effort to make submissions on the school to the RCOL. Unfortunately, this policy recommendation was shelved for fear of a public outcry. However, the community outcry from those whose children were being failed continued unabated. Pressure has been growing on the part of the community and critical educators to give serious consideration to these schools, as documented in my advocacy and extensive writings on the efficacy of the school in the Canadian context, in fact well before these recommendations were made public (Dei 1993, 1995, 1997; see also Dei 1996, 2008; Peters 2003). In a 2005 public forum when I (and others) made explicit reference to the school it was just a continuation of such advocacy that began in late 1970s and 1980s. In fact, our study of Dei et al. (1995, 1997) on Black youth school disengagement complemented findings school board indicating high dropout rates. Clyde McNeil's forum and editorial powerfully picked upon this long advocacy.

Multiple languages, along with multiple ways of knowing, seeing, and forming identity, also play key roles in African-centred schooling. The public hysteria over the Toronto District School Board's decision to approve an African-centred pilot school offers interesting lessons in moral panic. I maintain that it is a great day for Black and minority education in Canada to have a Board of Education officially support African-centred programming. It is a decision to throw a lifeline to students who otherwise have been disengaged/pushed out from the current school system. It is a decision to offer another chance at their education. Of course, we cannot interpret the decision to mean that the problem has been dealt with. The school must produce positive Results for the youth. The decision shows we have finally realized that we can no longer be seduced by the "sensation of moving while standing still". Condemning the idea in the face of continual youth failure in schools, especially while claiming that the current school system has within it the remedies to address the problem, is very hypocritical. The fact of the matter is that we have nothing to lose except to sit on our hands and not try something different. The system has not worked for our youth. We need to examine multiple strategies and options to ensure the success of our youth in schools.

Although successful examples of African-centred schools can be drawn from Detroit, Kansas, and Milwaukee, an instructive case emerges from the Oakland Unified School District. Established in 1992 as a programme for ninth grade students, the African-centred programme was inspired by the Ma'at values system from Egypt. The following core values are stressed: truth, justice, righteousness, propriety, balance, harmony, and order (Ginwright 2004: 89). The school strives to embed these values into curriculum delivery. For instance, how might we consider the omission and reclaiming of certain voices from official historic accounts, as seen in Chapter 2? How might truth, justice, and righteousness help our students to begin to ask about these omitted voices? How might our students be assisted and supported as they try to listen for and find these stories? Ongoing resistance by community members, challenges questioning the authenticity of African-centred knowledge, and the accessibility of this magnet programme endure; however, mainstream media reports equate the programme with state-sanctioned separation and racism.

In Ontario, considering the launch of a pilot African-centred elementary primary programme, Fall 2009, the community has been divided on the issue. It is to be expected. We are a very diverse community. However, like many others, I am disheartened by the negative portrayal of the community in discussions and debates over the proposal. As a community we are continually being told or lectured to take responsibility. Yet we think out solutions to the problems that afflict us and then get condemned. Where is all the outrage in the face of the failure of our youth? I find it interesting that in this supposed "crisis" in the Black community many misguidedly blame the "absence of fathers as role models in the homes". Yet, when we suggest the importance of the Black teachers in the African-centred school as important role models, we are asked: Does that really matter? We cannot have it both ways. Let us be honest.

Some opponents are genuinely concerned about "segregation". But is the school really about segregation? Others may point to dominant perceptions of the school. I would prefer that we are guided by the interests of the youth failed by the school system and not by what others think or say of the school or the youth. There is a lot of misinformation about the African-centred school proposal, notably the failure of opponents to read about alternative educational visions. Why would one call the school a "Black school" when as noted, the school is defined and guided more by the principles and ideas of African and Indigenous systems of thought. These include the following values: schooling as community; belongingness; responsibility to and respect for one's self, peers, community, and Elders; mutual interdependence; acknowledgement of all subject identities, including spiritual, racial, gender, sexual, cultural, ability, and linguistic diversity; an emphasis on the teachings of the sanctity of human life; a view of history as a totality of lived experience and its lessons; and the importance of achieving holistic success – academically, socially, and spiritually. Why is an idea for some students being interpreted as a proposal for *all* Black students? Why do some get a powerful urge to quarrel and vehemently oppose a pilot scheme to try out something different than the status quo? Whose interests are being defended? After all, if the pilot scheme works, the lessons can be transferred into mainstream schools to help all students. Most of us want integrated schools that work for all. It may be the ideal but we are not there yet. Before we get there we must grapple with integration – its benefits, costs, and expenses. Black solidarity cannot guarantee our students' success; at the time, however, integrated schools have been poor guarantors of success for our youth.

I have been reading media reports of some opponents branding those who favour such schools "crazy". Really? What about those who think we can simply sit on our hands and do nothing and hope everything will be fine. Schools have responded slowly to the request for inclusivity. Not to try something different in the face of overwhelming evidence that the system is not working for Black youth is to dispense with our ability to strategize. Are those who support the creation of Jewish schools, First Nations schools, Queer-focused schools, girls-only schools, and boys-only literacy classes also misguided?

The school can work with the needed resources, commitment, devotion, and patience. The school cannot be under-resourced to fail. It must have committed teachers. The community must be behind it and support it, including those who have doubts. The success of Black youth education is a success for all North American students.

The Yoruba of Nigeria have an important riddle: *What dines with the Oba* (a paramount chief of the community) *and leaves him to clear the dishes?* The answer: *the fly.* Those who comprise the "top" today, the ones most vocal in their opposition to the African-centred school, have been among those who have failed to act in very responsible ways with their power to ensure our schools work for all youth. Having dined with us they leave us to wash the dishes. On their way out they hypocritically blame, chastise, and show their arrogance in suggesting what we, as a community, should be thinking or doing. Rather than worry about segregation, we should first work to ensure that our schools are meeting the needs of all students. If they did, it is encouraging to note, we would not be talking about the need for African-centred schools in the first place!

Let me conclude by pleading with the community to support the school now and forget which side we have been on during the debate. We need to move on. The stakes are so high to remain divided when it comes to the education of our youth.

Role models matter. Black teachers, as role models, serve three purposes. First, these teachers may help to address the challenge of low teacher expectations of Black students. Research shows that this is a huge problem with the school system, one Black youth complain about (Dei et al. 1997). Second, there is the qualitative value of justice. In other words, it is only fair for students to see the teaching pool reflect the diversity around them so they can believe in themselves. It is an ethical and moral argument. In our research, students are clear in their comments: "We want to see more Black teachers!" and "I have never had a Black teacher!" (Dei et al. 1997: 3). We have a responsibility to hear these voices. But it is not to say any Black teacher. We need dedicated Black teachers and other allied educators. Why are we going through the trouble to ensure that our police force and media, for instance, reflect the diversity in our communities? We realize there is a valid public gain in this context. The idea of faculty and staff representation is intended to address the issue of diversity. Students know that excellence is reflected in the diversity that we have around us. Research shows many Black teachers have been successful in achieving excellence among Black students. Research in the United States, particularly from the Black colleges, shows this correlation (Allen 1985, 1992). The same is noted for all-girl schools with female teachers. The question of diverse staff representation is one out of many things in a complex web. Advocating for Black teachers in school systems is part of a package, provided other supports – curriculum reflective of the students' identities and realities, strong ties between the classroom and the wider communnity, and positive relationships between the students and teachers – are in place. But we cannot dismiss the voice of the students when they tell researchers they want to see more Black and minority teachers. The task is not simply to make excellence accessible but also equitable.

Third, African-centred schools are not race-centric. The school is defined more by its set of principles rather than by who attends or teaches there, including knowledge systems of community, responsibility, respect for Elders/authority, mutual interdependence, solidarity, and obligations to community and family, all of which borrow from African systems of thought. I prefer to call the school African-centered, *not* Black-focused; however, segments of the media have misinformed the public using "Black and race" to deflect from the genuine humanistic principles and ideas that guide the school. The only reason we would bring "Black-focus" to the debate again is to emphasize the demonstrated educational disadvantage that our students contend with in schools.

Fourth, how is performance being measured? Simply in academic and test scores? Do we bother to ask how students feel about being in a school as well? Do some students who "do well" in mainstream schools also sacrifice a bit of themselves, including their cultural identities? Do we achieve success, but at what costs? These are legitimate questions to ask.

8.6 Conclusion

We can in fact point to other successful African-centred schools in Chicago, Milwaukee, Kansas City, and Oakland. Notable examples include the Ladd School (elementary school in Missouri) and the African-centred Education Academy (an elementary school in Milwaukee). Let us not deny a legitimate call that African-centred schooling is a valid option that must be tried on a pilot basis. We are all searching for an answer to two systemic and endemic problems: Black disengagement and underachievement. We have not found an answer yet. It is foolhardy to say one option is not going to work when it has not been tried. What do we have to lose? Is it inclusion at all cost? If so, then at whose expense? Especially when such inclusion has not worked the way it has been implemented, African-centred schooling offers a compelling call to action and reflection. Aware of the salience of these contexts for knowledge production and interpretation, the concluding chapter considers the activist possibilities of African-centred schooling. Responding to the issues of community empowerment, health awareness, and sustainability, the discussion looks at the practical applications of teaching as anti-colonialism.

References

Allen, W. R. (1985) Black Student, White Campus: Structural, Interpersonal, and Psychological Correlates of Success. *Journal of Negro Education*, 54(2), 134–147.
Allen, W. R. (1992) The Color of Success: African-American College Student Outcomes at Predominantly Black Colleges. *Harvard Educational Review*, February, 62(1), 26–43.
Bhabha, H. (1994) *The Location of Culture*. London: Routledge.
Dei, G. J. S. (1993) Narrative Discourses of Black Parents and the Canadian Public School System. *Canadian Ethnic Studies*, 25(3), 45–65.
Dei, G. J. S. (1997) Beware of False Dichotomies: Revisiting the Idea of "Black-focused" Schools in Canadian Contexts. *Journal of Canadian Studies*, 31(4), 58–79.
Dei, G. J. S., Mazzuca, J., McIsaac, E. and Zine., J. (1997) Reconstructing "Dropout": A Critical Ethnography of the Dynamics of Black Students' Disengagement from Schools. Toronto: University of Toronto Press.
Ginwright, S. A. (2004) Black in School: African-Centred Reform, Urban Youth, and the Promise of Hip-Hop Culture. New York: Teacher's College Press.
Jhingram, D. (2007). "Language and Marginalization in Primary Education". Paper presented at the International Conference on: "School Education, Pluralism and Marginality". New Delhi. December 14–16.
Lattas, A. (1993) Essentialism, Memory and Resistance: Aboriginality and the Politics of Authenticity. *Oceania*, 63, 2–67.

Chapter 9
Looking to the Future – African-Centred Schooling in Action: Applying Development Discourse to Sustainability, Community Empowerment, and Health Awareness

Abstract This discussion concludes by making a case for African-centred theoretical and practical frameworks for development, sustainability, community empowerment, and health promotion. Resisting the entrenched Western construction of continental Africa as a recipient of aid, this discussion envisions means of effective development-as-agency. In seeking the authentic African self, the discussion makes a compelling case for contemporary notions of sustainability-as-political praxis. This activism has implications for equitable access to such social benefits as education and health promotion.

Keywords Practical applications · African-centred schooling · Development discourses · Community empowerment · Health awareness · Sustainability · Education for sustainability · Community-centred schooling · Partnership development · Educational possibilities

9.1 Introduction: Towards an Anti-colonial Prism of Development

Proud of my Ghanaian heritage, I come to the issue of African-centred schooling with a strong personal and professional politics and commitment. Writing this concluding chapter in the wake of the 50th anniversary of Ghana's independence from Britain, these ideas come at a very significant time in the annals of Ghana and, to speak broadly and emblematically, continental Africa.

Ghana recently witnessed a massive public resistance from local peoples and community groups – one sharply denied by the national government – to convert a national forest reserve into a commercial centre. The Achimota Forest, the only surviving green belt in the Accra metropolis, is to be sold to an entrepreneur who intends to build a shopping mall. This directive was said to have come from the Office of the President. Spanning over 900 acres, the land was designated as a Forest Reserve in 1930. Local critics have wondered why, at a time when many African countries without forests are turning certain portions of their cities into forests, Ghana is doing the reverse and selling off its natural forest in the capital city. I raise this example, one with personal implications, to illustrate the need for an embedded form of African-centred education and political engagement in practice. As we move beyond theory in this final chapter, I shall look at the praxis of our work in relation to empowered development: a linking of sustainability and community empowerment.

As noted the anti-colonial refers to an approach to theorizing colonial and re-colonial relations and the implications of imperial structures. These include the following aspects: processes of knowledge production and validation; the understanding of Indigeneity; the pursuit of agency, resistance, and subjective politics. Colonial, in this context, is understood as not simply "foreign" or "alien" but as "imposed" and "dominating" (Dei and Asgharzadeh 2001). By decolonization I refer to the intellectual, cultural, and political resistance of dominant ways of knowing and practices. This process is actual practice informing theory and vice versa. Situating decolonization in the anti-colonial project calls for the cultivation of one's identity and collective consciousness. Decolonization is an activity that also recognizes that the social processes of education are part of a dynamic process between different actors with unique and occasionally conflicting stakes in the outcome.

When applied to development practice, the decolonization project implies the following elements: shifting development away from a top-down approach to a bottom-up undertaking; asking questions about whose interests are being served; seeing local peoples as producers of knowledge; uncovering colonizing relations at the internal power dynamics of social relations, notably the asymmetrical power relations associated with race/ethnic, class, gender, linguistic, sexuality, and religious differences.

"Indigenousness" is about developing a local consciousness of one's existence: individually, socially, and collectively. Indigenous knowledge is knowledge associated with long-term occupancy of a place that allows a people to reference their own established cultural ways of knowing to resist imposition of "external" ideas and values. In African contexts, I am alluding to local fables, tales, and proverbs that are important sources of teaching and learning about society-culture and nature interface. When used strategically local/Indigenous knowledge becomes a strategic base from which to rupture our academies. My understanding of the notion of "indigenous" draws on the absence of colonial imposition. When applied to "development" we begin to see how such knowledge is about the power of local consciousness, local cultural resource base of African peoples, and their contributions to the development process, and the possibilities of multiple ways of knowing to bring about solution-oriented changes in people's lives and social reality.

The idea of spirituality and "spiritual knowing" as a substructure of development entails a shift in our understanding of spirituality beyond the aesthetic concerns of peace, love, humility, respect to what can be termed action-oriented revolutionary spirituality. In order to engage spirituality we must avoid the secular/sacred split, the material/non-material dichotomy, and the tendency to evade power issues in speaking about spirituality and multiple ways of knowing.

By enmeshing identity, spirituality, place, and Indigenous knowing as intrinsic elements of the self, students may be supported in their efforts to articulate and use their own anti-colonial frameworks. Teachers are encouraged to provide spaces for students to engage this framework by asking them to consider where knowledge and identity come from. Who are you? How would you define your identity? What messages do our families and communities give us about our identities? How do we use this knowledge in our daily lives? Why is it important to preserve this knowledge? Texts, resources, and activities featuring local Indigenous knowledge, including stories, games, and current news stories, are encouraged. Should these not be available, inviting guest speakers to share their insights is useful. Students may record and help to preserve this knowledge as well. While no single learning activity ensures that students frame their own anti-colonial framework, this approach provides spaces for activism and awareness.

9.2 Sustainability as Political and Intellectual Project

As a budding social anthropologist, my Ph.D. dissertation was entitled *Adaptation and Environmental Stress in Ghana*, a study of how local communities have survived socio-environmental and economic stressors, including drought, returning migrants, contraction in the national economy. While environmental degradation affects development, it is such unchecked economic growth, most notably presented in the guise of advancement, that causes the degradation in the first place. Debunking the poverty-environmental degradation thesis, poverty is not an independent variable. Poverty is not a predator or a destroyer of the environment. Environmental degradation is caused more by the ambitions of economic growth rather than by poverty (Escobar 1995). Tucker (1999: 1), referring to the "myth of development", contends that "the model of development now widely pursued is part of the problem rather than the solution." This Western ideology of development "distorts our imagination, limits our vision, [obscuring] us to the alternatives that human ingenuity is capable of imagining and implementing." In order to imagine new possibilities Southern peoples must deconstruct the myth of development using local and Indigenous cultural ways of knowing in an anti-colonial prism.

How we can better understand our relationships to environments and develop a critical consciousness of sustainability that is informed by key questions of power, social difference, equity, and justice? How do local cultural resource knowledges inform the rebuilding of environmentally and ecologically sound and sustainable communities? What are the social determinants of sustainability? It is imperative that we bring the social, spiritual, and cultural questions front and centre to our discussions on the environment and sustainability. I advocate the "socialization of the environment" through a focus on social justice and equity issues. I have been informed by a theorization of the environment beyond the physical/natural confines given the inseparability of nature, culture, and society. In framing "the social" in environment and sustainability discussions, the concern is not simply with the social contexts of the environment but also with how we address the social well-being of the planet. An important objective is to make the linkage between the current agendas for international development, equity issues, and global environments.

Teaching the social in environmental sustainability is to ensure that the educational, income, food, shelter, peace, security, equity, and social justice needs of all peoples are addressed. The environment is a human right and an equity issue (Selby et al. 1987; Bullard 1993; Warren et al. 1995; Escobar 1995; Munck and O'Hearn 1999; Garroutte 2003; McDonald 2004; Stein 2004; Kuenzi 2006; Jabareeen 2008). Recognizing that all peoples should have that fundamental right to a healthy planet, environmental care is a public good. The environment is more than a resource-based problem. It is equally important to also acknowledge the twin edge dimensions of environmental sustainability – the state of the environment is an important indicator of the level of "development" attained by a nation/community and how the environment contributes to make "development" possible. Only healthy people can contribute to the social, economic, and material progress of a society.

Jabareen (2008: 187) asserts that contemporary environmental discourse has been "globalized and transcended national boundaries" in the attempts to link debates about deforestation, climatic change, pollution, lack of biodiversity, and development issues. There is no single definition of sustainability; instead, there is the "fluid paradox of sustainability" (Jabareen 2008: 188). The idea of "sustainability" has become a very contested and value-laden notion. It is to be understood in a given political context with particular goals, priorities, and vested interests (Voinov 2008: 488).

Sustainability is about relations between humans and the use of resources. Sustainability also refers to stability of social and natural environments. It seeks to achieve a "balance" and "integrity" in use and renewal of social and natural resources; it encompasses an understanding of the relational dimensions of society, culture, and nature. Sustainability speaks to particular social-political arrangements. Voinov (2008: 497) also notes regional sustainability may be at odds with global sustainability. For the West, where the issue of conservation is now at the top of the development agenda, sustainability may be an enticing discussion. However, in the South, where sustainability has always been part of local cultural knowledge and social practice, there is nothing new. Hence, the cultural and political dimensions are integral parts of discussing sustainability. Sustainability refers to the ability to maintain balance between enduring social, cultural, and natural interrelations so as to ensure effective use and regeneration of social and physical resources.

Indigenous conceptions of sustainability speak of "a particular Cosmo vision of Indigenous peoples who understand nature as a whole, as life itself. Therefore nature cannot be instrumentalized on the grounds of further material gains. Nature is mediated by ethic principles that are grounded, simultaneously, in cultural values built along centuries of harmonic coexistence with and within nature" (Osorio et al. 2005: 504). Jabareen (2008) has noted that sustainability can no longer be an "environmental logo" We must look at sustainability from the point of view of society and power relations rather than the environment. Let us consider the extent to which sustainability can be achieved without the "effective balancing of social, economic and environmental objectives" (Jabareen 2008: 183). "Intergenerational" and "intragenerational" equity are central to sustainability: the "fair allocation of resources between current and future generations"…. and the "equitable distribution of power [and resource] that can contribute to improvements in environmental quality" (Jabareen 2008: 184).

Recognizing that environmental health cannot be separated from progressive – and African-centred – development, Munck and O'Hearn (1999) contend that much of the ongoing intellectual discussion on "development" is caught in the dominant paradigms of Western thinking. Alternative visions and counter theoretical perspectives of development even struggle to disentangle from the dominance of the Eurocentric paradigm. Eurocentrism is intrinsic in the ways we think, conceptualize, and organize knowledge about the environment. The whole debate about environmental sustainability has been shaped by the cultural forces and the political agendas of the West (Tucker 1999).

Tucker (1999) and Prah (1997) in their excellent critique of "development" have argued that the West has the definitional power to control development discourse. The same can be applied to conventional ways of talking about the environment: the tendency to blame local peoples' cultural practices, customs, traditional values, attitudes, and beliefs as obstacles to environmental sustainability. No attempt is made to interrogate the Eurocentric, capital-driven development strategies. Considering African-centred development, the local cultural resource knowledges of African peoples have been the least analysed for their contribution to the national development process.

Africa has been a rich source of data that has helped ground important theories about our social world, human condition, and the disciplines. And, at the same time, Africa and African knowledges are devalued in our academies. Those who seek to write about and understand Africa may not have embodied connections to the continent. Unfortunately, these scholars/researchers are given the discursive and authorial power in such a way that renders African peoples as being without knowledge. I am speaking of the insulting idea that others know us better, as Africans, or more than we know ourselves (Prah 1997).

The control of development discourse is further entrenched by the "imperial saviour": Africa as a site of confusion and chaos. Africa is rendered impure through the white gaze. In such discussions "Whiteness" and purity as racial identities contribute to "valid" knowledge production about "development" (Warren et al. 1995; Taiaiake and Corntassel 2005; Jabareen 2008). Social identities significantly implicate how development experts and practitioners come to produce, validate, and use "knowledge" about marginalized communities. Africa continues to be saddled with the untold hardships on its local populations through World Bank and IMF-inspired structural adjustment policies that emphasize cost-effectiveness, downloading unto parents and communities.

Investigations of the differential impact of environmental degradation and crisis on racialized populations reveal disturbing trends. Big companies dumping industrial waste disproportionately affect the least advantaged segments of our populations (First National People of Colour Environmental Leadership Summit 1991). In urban centres and rural areas, a class analysis helps to identify lower income subjects as having lower levels of vision, hearing, and speech; higher infant mortality rates; homes in less safe neighbourhoods; higher incidents of mental disorders; higher rates of exposure to environmental contaminants. Indigenous and racialized communities, the poor, children, and the elderly are often disproportionately affected by toxic pollutants (Bullard 1993; Gosine and Teelucksingh 2008; Nath 2008). Further, the children of racialized poor women are disproportionately exposed to a heavier burden of toxic contaminants. Gosine and Teelucksingh (2008) argue popular environmentalisms are informed by whiteness. The real power of Western "popular environmentalism" lies in its definitional and discursive power. It controls the production of knowledge about the planet and flexes discursive muscle to regulate environmental thought and practice.

9.3 Rethinking Sustainability: The Quest for Education for Sustainability

Indigenousness includes a knowledge consciousness that comes from the long-term occupancy of a place. Indigenousness is engaged as the nexus of culture, society, and culture. Spirituality then becomes a knowledge base grounded in the understanding of local environments: the land as sacred and the sacredness of activity thereupon it. Recognizing the dynamism of culture, place/land, identity, and knowledge, the evocation of the environment/land is in contestations over history, language, identity and heritage.

The land is so important in informing us that the "objective knowledge of the physical environment" is different from experiencing the physical environment "in the flesh", subjective knowledge about the environment. The objective analysis of the environment does not fully equip one to understand the actual experience of engaging the environment. This is a form of knowledge that is embodied. It is not rooted in biology but arises from social experiences of a subject/body in a context where such knowledge about the environment is salient. How Indigenous peoples come to understand and work with " the entities of nature, plants, animals, stones, trees, mountains, rivers, lakes and a host of living entities...all constitute embodied relationships that must be respected" (Cajete 2000: 78).

The "environmental crisis" is a product of modernity (Reznai-Moghaddam and Karami 2008: 408). Education for sustainability should move beyond the duality of the physical and social to a more holistic conceptualization of the environment: natural, physical, and social spaces. The environment is a spiritual and cultural resource knowledge. Distinguishing between the environment as a resource and as a site of knowledge production, there is theoretical and methodological blindness when we focus on one and not the other. The issue of embodied knowing/embodiment is understood fundamentally as part of the living and the connections of the physical and metaphysical realms of existence. We need to ask a new question: Is sustainability as currently conceptualized, a "privileged discourse" – sustainability for whom, why, and how?

Education for sustainability plays a critical role as we determine answers to the preceding question. In providing spaces for student engagement and activism, education for sustainability should be more than educating to sustain human lives.

Such education should also work with the uncertainty of knowing: the ontological primacy of interpretations – how we make sense of our worlds and the resources for knowing about the environment. "Environmental sustainability" must take into account local understandings of the workings of culture, society, and nature. The emotional and spiritual well-being of the individual and the social group is the bedrock of any "environmental sustainability" process. Environmental sustainability means matching individual rights of group membership with corresponding collective responsibilities. To deal with power inequities that exist in our communities to create environmentally sustainable societies, and not to evade the power issues and the problematic separation of the material and the non-material, we must engage in a "project of restoration". This is the restoring of hope, vision, and the dreams of communities (Kuenzi 2006).

To cite one timely example, the project of restoration is also reflected in community efforts to provide access to education, both formally and informally. Recognizing the often-prohibitive nature of education, including fees for uniforms, tuition, and school supplies, as well as cultural barriers for female students in some contexts, non-formal Education (NFE) has played a major role in making education accessible to rural citizens.

The World Bank dominates the development discourse rather than via the money it provides – or fails to provide – for development. Such observations are important because they reinforce a long-standing critique of the conventional development discourse and practice and also raise questions about who controls the discourse of development and why? A critical review of Structural Adjustment Programs (SAPs), World Bank-financed loans with often high and penalizing interest rates and restructuring requirements, using Foucault's analysis of power, knowledge, and discourse shows how "development" is actually about extending Western disciplinary and normalizing mechanisms to dominate the South (Djokoto 2002). The real power of World Bank/IMF lies in its definitional power, its control over the production of knowledge about development, its ability to use discursive muscle to regulate the development thought and practice. In fact, SAPs reshape development to reflect a particular political and economic agenda. I see this model as characterized by the free markets and the free trade movement.

Sustainability and development provide opportunities for teachers to engage students in these debates. Invite students to define their own definitions of what sustainability and development should look like for their communities: how and where should people live, how will they earn their livelihoods, how will they gain access to health care and education, and how empowered will the community be? How do these visions of sustainability and development differ from current practices? Using research strategies, including data gathering via critical reading, observations, and interviews, ask students to prepare a sustainability and development plan for their community, one incorporating Indigenous knowledge and practices. As part of civic engagement and active citizenship, have students present their findings to community leaders. In moving the sustainability and development debate and activism beyond the classroom, students are empowered to consider these issues in relation to their own lives and in connection with the health of their communities.

9.4 Building Healthy and Sustainable Communities: The Challenges and Possibilities

Along with education, there is a profound health divide that is evident between the North and the South. Today, nearly all child deaths occur in developing countries, almost half of them in Africa. We are told that of the 20 countries in the world with the highest child mortality (probability of death under 5 years of age), 19 are in Africa, the exception being Afghanistan. Women in developing countries are more than 100 times more likely to die of pregnancy-related causes than their counterparts in industrialized countries. Twenty-five per cent of the population in developing countries and countries in transition lack access to clean drinking water, and less than half have access to adequate sanitation. More than 350 million children and adults are suffering from malnutrition. The gap in life expectancy between the richest and poorest countries is more than 30 years. HIV/AIDS is eroding the health and development gains of the previous 50 years in many countries, leading to significant declines in life expectancy. Tuberculosis (TB) is the leading killer of people infected with HIV, and up to 50% of people with HIV or AIDS develop TB. These troubling statistics reveal the need for a critical understanding of "access to health" as a defining element of what constitutes "development" (see also Editor 2004).

We know that historically many Southern countries have been working to create self-reliant models of development under the framework of people-centred national policies. In the area of health, many remarkable advances were made. For example, China's "barefoot doctor" model was based on community-led health initiatives. People-centred approaches to health, ones focusing on the larger socioeconomic causes of illness, including reduced access to food, housing, and education, have met with success in Ghana, South Africa, and Zambia (van der Borne 2006; Robson and Sylvester 2007; Luginaah 2008).

To use the dominant construction of HIV/AIDS as an example, the focus on this disease is taking a huge portion of the health sector resources in Africa. As Luginaah (2008) also notes, AIDS has become a trope for constructing of Africa as the "Other". While not exclusive to Africa, HIV/AIDS is generally seen as a major health problem in every part of the continent. Resources are being directed to places even where the disease is not the primary health problem. I say this not to diminish the seriousness of HIV/AIDS but to make clear the problem of misplaced priorities and contestations of knowledge. Community-based solutions, particularly to HIV/AIDS, are yielding promising Results (Camlin 2008; van der Borne 2006; Robson and Sylvester 2007).

There are other unheralded struggles at social transformation in health in a number of communities in the South. We need to capture these. Primary Health Care (PHC) has always been the cornerstone of community self-reliance. In most countries where PHC was adopted through an Indigenous development framework, it is enmeshed as part of the local and national fabric.

The failures of PHC can be attributed in part to the fact that the biomedical model is still privileged in health development initiatives – particularly the continuing focus on disease-oriented, curative measures and health professionals trained in the biomedical framework (Luginaah 2008). Health development cannot be imposed from above. A "people-centred health intervention" is called for, one in which local peoples themselves become active participants in their own health care and development.

Effective community participation will allow local subjects to articulate their health issues and concerns through critical consciousness about health matters while working with state and international support to find home-grown solutions in ways that are culturally, politically, and economically congruent and meaningful to local peoples. Health development focus must shift from the top-down, capital intensive, technology-based, curative-oriented, disease-focused, and mostly urban-based health system to preventive, local technology, knowledge, and skills and grassroot-based approach to health development. For genuine health development there must be less dependence on foreign capital and external health expertise.

In order to heal our communities, we need to work with the synergy of body, mind, and soul; to speak of our "community" as a community of differences, to recognize the multiple subjectivities that make up each of our communities (race, class, gender, ability, and sexuality as extremely consequential for engaging society). We must deal with power inequities that exist in our communities to create healthy societies and not to evade the power issues and the problematic separation of the material and the non-material. This activism helps to provide hope, vision, and the dreams of youth. The provision of basic support systems, services, and infrastructural support provides the capacity for every member of our community to contribute to the production of the valued goods and services of society and to benefits from their sacrifices.

Fostering community affords opportunities for African-centred teaching. Our students benefit from looking and experiencing community through a variety of strategies. Invite students to look at traditional and mainstream methods of healing in their communities. How are these approaches similar and different? How might the two approaches be brought together? Why is it important to preserve local forms of healing? Interviews with community leaders, healers, and patients provide opportunities for students to see and, hopefully, defend traditional medicines as expressions of identity, place, and community.

9.5 Looking Forward to Reframe Development

Nwoye (2006) urges us to reclaim the African self. Looking inwards, listening to the silenced and embodied knowledge, offers the promise for African-centred development. Recalling the deforestation near Accra, an example of disempowering and ill-advised "development" cited at the beginning of this chapter, we see the relevance of our activism around locally informed and progressive development. Whether the development initiative is related to sustainability, accessible education, health promotion, or other social goals, the stakes are high. As a multifaceted process, development must take into account local understandings of the workings of culture, society, and nature. The emotional and spiritual well-being of the individual and the social group is the bedrock of any development process. Social development means matching individual rights of group membership with corresponding social responsibilities. Our children, along with the allies of African-centred schooling and development, deserve nothing less.

References

Bullard, R. D. (Ed.) (1993) Confronting Environmental Racism: Voices from the Grassroots. Boston: South End Press.
Cajete, G. (2000) *Native Science: Natural Laws of Interdependence*. Santa Fe: Clear Light Publishers.
Camlin, C. (2008) Parental Investment, Club Membership, and Youth Sexual Risk Behavior in Cape Town. *Health Education Behavior*, 35(4), 522.
Dei, G. and Asgharzadeh., A. (2001) The Power of Social Theory: The Anti-colonial Discursive. *Journal of Educational Thought*, 35(3), 297–323.
Djokoto, J. (2002). Transitional problems in the vertical progression of students between the secondary school and the university in Swaziland. *Education Futures and New Citizenships*. The 10th National Biennial Conference of the Australian Curriculum Studies Association. Canberra, 29 September – 1 October 2001. Australian Curriculum Studies Association, www.acsa.edu.au/2001conf/.
Editor (2004) The Global Assault on Health. *Peoples Health Movement*. http://www.phmovement.org/pubs/issuepapers/hong16.html
Escobar, A. (1995) Encountering Development. The Making and Unmaking of the Third World. New Jersey: Princeton University Press.
First National People of Colour Environmental Leadership Summit. (1991) *Proceedings of the First National People of Colour Environmental Leadership Summit*. Washington, DC: First National People of Colour Environmental Leadership Summit.
Garroutte, E. M. (2003) *Real Indians: Identity and Survival of Native Americans*. Berkeley: University of California Press.
Gosine, A. and Teelucksingh., C. (2008) *Environmental Justice and Racism in Canada: An Introduction*. Toronto: Emond Montgomery.
Jabareen, Y. (2008) A New Conceptual Framework for Sustainable Development. *Environment, Development and Sustainability*, 10, 179–192.
Kuenzi, M. (2006) Non-formal Education and Community Development in Senegal. *Community Development Journal*, 41(2), 210–222.
Luginaah, I. (2008) Local gin (*akpeteshie*) and HIV/AIDS in the Upper West Region of Ghana: The Need for Preventive Health Policy. *Health & Place*, 14(4), December 2008, 806–816.
McDonald, D. A. (2004). *Environmental Justice in South Africa*. Juta Academic.
Munck, R. and O'Hearn, D. (Eds.) (1999) Critical Development Theory: Contributions to the New Paradigm. London: Zed Books.
Nath, B. (2008) A Heuristic for Setting Effective Standards to ensure Global Environmental Sustainability. *Environment, Development and Sustainability*, 10, 471–486.
Nwoye, A. (2006) Remapping the Fabric of the African Self: A Synoptic Theory. *Dialectical Anthropology*, 30, 119–146.
Osorios, L., Lobato, M. and Del Castillo., A. (2005) Debates on Sustainable Development: Towards a Holistic View of Reality. *Environment, Development and Sustainability*, 7, 501–518.
Prah, K. K. (1997) Beyond the Color line: Pan-Africanist Disputations, Selected Sketches, Letters, Papers, and Reviews. Trenton, NJ: Africa World Press.

References

Reznai-Moghaddam, K. and Karami, E. (2008) A Multiple Criteria Evaluation of Sustainable Agricultural Development Models Using AHP. *Environment, Development and Sustainability.*, 10, 407–426.

Robson, S. and Sylvester, K. B. (2007) Orphaned and Vulnerable Children in Zambia: The Impact of the HIV/AIDS Epidemic on Basic Education for Children at Risk. *Educational Research*, 49(3), 259–272.

Selby, D., Grieg, S. and Pike., G. (1987). *Earthrights: Education as if the Planet Really Mattered.* Kogan Page/World Life Fund.

Stein, R. (2004) New Perspectives on Environmental Justice: Gender, Sexuality, and Activism. New York: Rutgers University Press.

Taiaiake, A. and Corntassel., J. (2005) Being Indigenous: Resurgences Against Contemporary Colonialism. *Government and Opposition*, 40(4), 597–614.

Tucker, V. (1999) The Myth of Development: A Critique of a Eurocentric Discourse. In Munck, R. and O'Hearn, D. (Eds.) *Critical Development Theory: Contributions to the New Paradigm.* London: Zed Books.

van den Borne, B. (2006) Impact of an HIV and AIDS Life Skills Program on Secondary School Students in Kwazulu-Natal. *South Africa AIDS Education and Prevention*, 18(4), 281–294.

Voinov, A. (2008) Understanding and Communicating Sustainability: Global Versus Regional Perspectives. *Environment Development and Sustainability*, 10, 487–501.

Warren, D. M.; Slikkerveer, L. J. and Brokensha, D., (Eds.) (1995) *The Cultural Dimension of Development: Indigenous Knowledge Systems.* London: Intermediate Technology Publications.

Index

A
Advocacy, 105, 108
Africa, 2–4, 6–9, 19–24, 33–44, 47–59, 61–70, 76, 80, 83–84, 96, 103, 117, 121, 124
African-centred development, 74, 121
African-centred education, 19–22, 37–44, 115, 118
African-centred schooling, 40–42, 111, 115–126
African development, 48–49, 56, 59, 62–65, 74, 80–81
African history, 6–7, 13, 15–31, 33, 55–56, 110
African knowledges, 121
African local knowledges, 59, 77
Anti-colonial education, 34, 54, 57–58, 89–105
Anti-colonialism, 57, 116

B
Bias, 1, 7, 62, 111

C
Case study, 73
Challenging the Africanist, 9, 38, 42–43, 103
Claiming power, 104
Community-centred schooling, 117
Community empowerment, 116–126
Contemporary learner, 7, 107–116
Critical education, 37–38, 54, 107–111
Critical theory, 73
Curriculum, 10, 16–17, 23, 28–29, 41–43, 57, 84, 103, 111–112, 115
Curriculum design, 15
Curriculum expectations, 10, 28
Curriculum omissions, 41

D
Decolonization, 6, 13, 38, 61–70, 100, 103, 118

Development, 2, 4, 6–7, 35, 43, 48–49, 52, 54–57, 61–70, 73–86, 96, 100, 117–126
Development discourses, 117
Diversity, 7, 16, 36, 39, 41, 54, 58, 69, 77, 81, 83, 96, 107, 110–111, 114–115, 120
Diversity of continental Africa, 47
Du Bois, 19–20, 40, 50–52, 92, 103

E
Educational possibilities, 117
Education for sustainability, 122–123
Educators, 13, 16, 34–35, 37, 41, 43, 54–55, 81–83, 85–86, 109–111, 115
Effective social change, 73
Equity, 6, 17, 35, 41–43, 46, 58, 90, 95, 98–100, 108, 110–111, 119–120

G
Ghana, 1, 8, 12, 51, 117, 119, 124

H
Health awareness, 116–126
Holistic education, 33

I
Identity, 34, 37–40, 42–43, 49, 57, 64, 69, 75–77, 90–91, 98–103, 107–111, 118–119, 122, 125
Identity formation, 33, 61, 64
Identity production, 89
Indigeneity, 34–35, 91–93, 97–103, 118
Indigenous knowledge, 44, 62, 69, 73–86, 89–105, 118–119, 123
Infused curriculum, 107
Integrative theory, 33–44
Interconnections, 74, 79, 103

K
Knowledge formation, 61
Knowledge production, 34–35, 38, 54, 58, 69, 78, 85–86, 90, 92, 94, 98–103, 116

L
Learning, 2–4, 6, 11, 15–31, 33–36, 38, 41–44, 48, 54–55, 57, 78, 80–83, 97, 102, 104, 110–111, 118–119
Learning activities, 11, 29–30
Learning strategies, 1
Learning tools, 89
Locality, 63
Localization, 47
Local knowledges, 34, 59, 75, 77, 83

O
Ontario curriculum, 17
Oral history, 2–4

P
Partnership development, 117
Pedagogy, 41, 43, 57, 85, 90, 103
Philosophy, 17, 37–44, 51, 74, 76–77, 83
Political activism, 49
Politicization, 107
Power dynamics, 118
Practical applications, 31, 116
Practice, 2, 11, 16–17, 22, 30, 34–37, 39, 41, 50, 64, 69–70, 74–77, 80, 93, 95, 98, 102–103, 118

Q
Questioning, 73, 109, 113

R
Resistance, 6–7, 24, 34, 38, 42, 48, 55–56, 85–86, 90, 92, 95, 99, 101, 103, 108, 113
Responsive school programming, 107

S
Silenced histories, 47
Social progress, 73
Student engagement, 122
Students, 7, 10–13, 15–19, 27–31, 36, 41–43, 47–48, 50, 55–58, 81–83, 93–95, 109–115
Sustainability, 59, 116–126

T
Teaching, 2–4, 6, 15–31, 33–38, 41–44, 48, 54–59, 61–70, 80, 82–84, 94, 110–111, 114–115
Teaching and learning processes, 89
Teaching as resistance, 47
Theory, 19–21, 30, 33–44, 48, 53, 63, 66, 80, 98, 102, 118

U
United States, 2–3, 10, 18, 20, 22–23, 25–26, 28, 50, 52, 91, 115

Lightning Source UK Ltd.
Milton Keynes UK
UKOW021851040212

186682UK00003B/4/P